A Zen Wave

The cover incorporates a fourteenth-century ink painting by Kaŏ (reproduced on p. 136).

ROBERT AITKEN

A ZEN WAVE

Bashō's Haiku and Zen

New York·WEATHERHILL·*Tokyo*

First edition, 1978

Published by John Weatherhill, Inc., of New York and Tokyo, with
editorial offices at 7–6–13 Roppongi, Minato-ku, Tokyo 106, Japan.
Protected by copyright under terms of the International Copyright
Union; all rights reserved. Printed in the Republic of Korea and first
published in Japan.

LIBRARY OF CONGRESS CATALOGING IN PUBLICATION DATA: Aitken,
Robert, 1917– / A Zen wave / 1. Matsuo, Bashō, 1644–1694—
Criticism and interpretation. / 2. Zen Buddhism in literature. / 3.
Matsuo Bashō, 1644–1694—Religion and ethics. / I. Matsuo, Bashō,
1644–1694. / II. Title. / PL794.4.Z5A78 / 895.6'1'3 / 78–13243 /
ISBN 0–8348–0137–X pbk.

for Anne

Contents

Illustrations will be found
on the following pages:
33–34, 51–52, 117–18, 135–36

Acknowledgments

I OWE ANY INSIGHT I may have to Yamada Kōun Rōshi, Abbot of the Sanbō Kyōdan Sect of Zen Buddhism, Kamakura, Japan. I am most grateful for his rigorous and compassionate guidance. I also owe much to the late Yasutani Hakuun Rōshi, whose inspired and steadfast encouragement helped all of us at the Diamond Sangha to establish our Zen practice, and to Nakagawa Sōen Rōshi, whose own way of haiku and Zen showed me how the two are not separate. My deep thanks are also due to the late Professor R. H. Blyth, who was like a father in helping me to find my life path.

I am very grateful to students at the two centers of the Diamond Sangha, Koko An Zendo and Maui Zendo, for their supportive interest when these chapters were talks at our Sunday meetings. In particular, I wish to thank P. Nelson Foster for his editorial assistance in the work of rendering the talks into essays for our journal, *Blind Donkey*. He also read through the manuscript of the present book and made many helpful suggestions, as did W. S. Merwin and Anne Aitken. I stole good ideas from Gary Snyder and Ryo Imamura, and received further help from Yamada Rōshi, Maezumi Taizan Rōshi, Tetsugen Glassman Sensei, Miyazaki Kan'un Rōshi, Paul Shepherd, Marshall P. S. Wu, and members of the Zen Center of Los Angeles.

The illustration *A Goblin Chanting Buddha's Name* is reproduced by permission of the Honolulu Academy of Arts, gift of John Wyatt Gregg Allerton, 1952. *The Priest Hsien-tzu,* by Kaō (collection of Shoji Hattori, Tokyo), *Violets,* by Bashō, and the detail of *Evening Rain,* by Bashō (Masaki Museum), are reproduced by permission of Heibonsha. *Chuang-tzu and the Butterfly,* by Taiga, is reproduced by courtesy of the owners, Kurt and Millie Gitter, the photo of the Bashō image by courtesy of David Salemme, the photo of Yamada Rōshi by courtesy of Donald Stoddard, and the photo of Yasutani Rōshi by courtesy of the Zen Center of Los Angeles.

Portions of Fumiko Fujikawa's "The Influence of Tu Fu on Bashō" are quoted with permission of *Monumenta Nipponica.* "That" by Joyce Carol Oates is quoted by permission of *The Nation.* "You be Bosatsu, . . ." is quoted from Gary Snyder, *Earth House Hold,* copyright 1969 by Gary Snyder. Reprinted by permission of New Directions Publishing Corporation. "Preludes I" is quoted from *Collected Poems 1909–1962* by T. S. Eliot, copyright 1936 by Harcourt Brace Jovanovich, Inc.; copyright 1963, 1964 by T. S. Eliot. Reprinted by permission of the publishers. The same poem, "Preludes I," is quoted by permission of Faber and Faber Ltd., for reprinting in countries other than the U.S.A.

Foreword

THERE HAVE BEEN a number of translations of Bashō's haiku into English in this century—works of varying scope, emphasis, and interest—including one by Robert Aitken's own early guide both in the study of Japanese literature and of Zen, R. H. Blyth. But there has been no presentation of Bashō's work, and the experience of which it is a manifestation, in terms of the particular cast of Bashō's religious insight into his world and ours. To underestimate this aspect of Bashō's writing and his life is to risk missing what he himself evidently took to be the center of them both, the essence of his nature and his art, and the secret of the relation between them. The history of his relation to the actual tradition of Zen, insofar as it is known, is a matter for his biographers. Recognition and appreciation of the certainty and depth of Bashō's realization, on the other hand, require not only a knowledge of the historical and literary context, but an ear for the poetry. And this recognition and appreciation would stand to benefit from a clear and authoritative familiarity with that sense, that way, referred to as Zen, that is neither in the words nor absent from them.

Robert Aitken's whole life appears to have been a maturing of both provisions. Brought up in Hawaii, his love for poetry and his fascination with Japanese culture were with him from his early youth. At the beginning of World War II he was on Guam in a civilian capacity, and was picked up by the Japanese and interned for the duration of the war. It was in the internment camp at Kobe in 1944 that he met Blyth and studied with him. After the war he took a degree in English literature, did graduate work in Japanese at the University of Hawaii, and began Zen practice with Nyogen Senzaki in California. In 1950 he returned to Japan on a grant to study haiku poetry, and to practice as a lay resident at the Zen monastery of Ryūtaku-ji, in Mishima, under Yamamoto Gempō Rōshi and Nakagawa Sōen Rōshi. His study of both subjects has continued ever since. The concern with haiku poetry focused early on its greatest exemplar, Bashō—the working out of a deep sympathy. And the Zen practice led him to the Sanbō Kyōdan lineage of Zen Buddhism, and the teachers Yasutani Hakuun Rōshi and Yamada Kōun Rōshi. The latter, who is the present abbot of the order, conferred on Robert Aitken the title of independent rōshi—or venerable Zen master—in 1974, making him one of the first American Zen rōshi.

The migration of the transmission of Zen to the United States that has been going on for almost a century can be seen as a continuing act of translation. There have been in the past, and there now are, Zen masters born in Japan whose command of English has been astonishing. But of course, if Zen is really to take root in our culture, American-born teachers will have to emerge. Zen did not begin in Japan—or Korea—and ultimately is not a matter of one culture or one language, any more than poetry is. The translation of Zen, the translation of poetry, the translation that is poetry, appear to have so much in common as to suggest a common root, a single impulse of which they are aspects. Blyth himself went so far as to say that Zen *is* poetry, while neatly—or at least rhetorically—and wisely avoiding a definition of either. The attention and importance accorded to poetry—and to the spontaneous formality of the arts in general—in Japanese Zen is known to everyone in the West who has dipped into any level of Zen literature in English, and it seems perfectly appropriate that these commentaries by an American Zen master on the essential nature of Bashō's poetry should have been given, originally, as talks to Zen students.

Everyone who uses translation is reminded regularly that all translation, however the word may be construed, is impossible. We have to accept this, and we have to recognize also that translation of poetry, and translation of Zen, contribute barriers of their own to this basic absolute impossibility. But once we have admitted this, we must set it aside if we wish to read translation—or anything at all. For art itself is not altogether possible (it is one of the things about it that we prize), and yet it exists, for all that—just as we live not only in the absolute but at the same time in the world of the necessary and the possible. And in making our practical, relative choice, we are doing what Zen masters in China a thousand years ago felt they had to do in order to teach at all. For what they were impelled to transmit, they all agreed, was utterly unteachable: the Absolute, by definition undefinable, unnamable, and beyond experience itself, since there could not properly be said to be an experiencer of "it." It remained in the dimension of the Absolute they referred to as "the primary." "The secondary," then, was the reemergence into relativity, distinction, phenomena, practice, words—into means that might indicate their own invisible and inexpressible origin. One sentence in the *Diamond Sutra,* a sentence of crucial importance in the early evolution of the Zen tradition, reads: "Mind that abides nowhere must come forth." Something of the kind happens in—something of the kind *is*—the translation of poetry. There is no way really to say what the source, the original, is. The closer one looks, the more completely it vanishes. Yet no one who can read it, certainly no one who loves it, ever doubts that it is there. How can one represent "it?" And will a representation represent a second, or a first time?

One does not have to know Japanese to become aware that the translation of haiku into English poses special problems that cannot be explained away merely by describing them as linguistic and cultural. One of these is simply the form itself. Whatever life, associations, strength, and poetry of the original words may be lost or reborn in translation, the Western reader seems frequently to bring to translations of haiku preconceptions that are of no help at all. Any distinct form of an art implies a characteristic vision of completeness, and the completeness of the haiku form, as Bashō perfected it, is not just a matter of brevity and the emphatic arrangement of the seventeen syllables. One Western reader said that going through a collection of haiku was like being pecked to death by doves. It was not, I imagine, merely that the poems were so short that they seemed to end before they had satisfactorily begun, but that expectations of a recognizable development had been consistently frustrated. Haiku are often printed in series, whether they were written that way or not, thus inviting expectations of still other kinds of development that the reading of a sequence may not satisfy. It is true that the form, as it came to Bashō and as he sometimes used it, was part of a convention of linked verse in which every poem echoed or alluded to an aspect of its predecessor in a way that embodied definite rules. But I suspect that the Western reader's disappointment with the haiku collection would not have been allayed by an understanding of that convention. I would guess that it arises from precisely what Bashō himself wanted the form, each instance of it, to be. Not static, as the unsympathetic Western reader might suppose. But dynamic in the manner of a single frame of thought—an instant that is unique, indivisible, and therefore, whole. The flash itself, immeasurable in any time whatever: no-time manifesting in time. So the moment of the haiku could be said not to move but to be, totally, movement: that movement which, because it is not relative, is inseparable from stillness. The movement in stillness of the thing itself, not concepts of it; not, as Wallace Stevens put it, ideas about it. It is oneness in that sense that Bashō means to present in each poem. The sound of the frog, not as an image of the universe, but as the universe, as Bashō, as each one who hears it, in the moment of hearing. And nothing else, because there can be nothing else.

Thus the profound intimacy of this poetry into which the the postures and qualifications and noise of an "I" obtrude relatively so little. And thus again the blood relation with the insight of Zen, which one master saw as "a jet black iron ball speeding through the dark night." That is the stillness of Bashō's haiku.

It is a clear sense of these aspects of Bashō's poetry that Aitken Rōshi has set out to represent, not only in English but in "the secondary"—for his whole commentary is an extension of his translation, a part of it, and emphasizes the kind of fidelity to the original that he hoped to provide. With a plainness, a lack of ostentation, and at the same time an authority that are the fruits of years of study, he tells us poem by poem what to listen for and how to listen to Bashō, and to ourselves.

W. S. MERWIN

Introduction

IN 1950 I SUBMITTED an M.A. dissertation titled "Bashō's Haiku and Zen" to the University of Hawaii. I do not consider that work adequate today, but I learned much from writing it, and an admonition from a member of my thesis committee, Cheuk-woon Taam, stands out in my mind. He said that just because its subject is everywhere, I must be careful not to claim universal manifestation for Zen Buddhism.

Professor Taam's words are very much to the point. Zen Buddhism does not pervade the cosmos. It presents essential nature—universal mind—but it does so as a particular teaching. Confusing the specific teaching with its vast and undifferentiated subject is a trap that has caught several tigers.

About a century ago, Imakita Kōsen, an illustrious master of Engaku Monastery in Kamakura, Japan, commented on the recorded sayings of Confucius and Mencius in a collection titled *Zenkai Ichiran* (One Wave of the Zen Sea), in which he taught Zen by using examples from the *Analects* and the *Doc-*

trine of the Mean.[1] His purpose was not, I am sure, to show that world culture is an ocean named Zen, of which Confucianism is one wave, but rather that Chinese social philosophy is a particular formulation of essential nature that helps to reveal the truths of Zen. I take his work as my inspiration and precedent. Bashō's haiku express essential nature vividly, and my effort will be to reveal Zen through them as yet another wave of the great mind ocean that pervades all things.

Historically, it is possible to show that Matsuo Bashō took private instruction from the Priest Butchō, a Zen master who lived near him in Edo (present Tokyo). Moreover, at least two of Bashō's students practiced *zazen* (Zen meditation) under teachers of their own. However, we do not seem to find him recommending zazen to anyone, even as an adjunct to the writing of poetry.[2] He wore the robes of a Zen Buddhist monk, but this was no more than a convention of haiku poets of his period. It would be clearly wrong to claim Bashō as a Zen poet in the sense that George Herbert was a Christian poet.

Upon examining his haiku themselves, one can find evidence of Zen influence occasionally in the terminology. For example, he included the line "*ge no hajime* [beginning of the summer retreat]" in one of his haiku, using a seasonal reference that is generally limited to monastic vocabulary.[3] This shows that Bashō was familiar with the ways of Zen monks to some degree, but it is thin evidence for a case to establish Zen as anything more than an element in his environment.

With reference to subject matter, Bashō is sometimes called a nature poet. However, as Donald Keene points out, while Bashō wrote of the natural world and was deeply affected by it, his motivation to write and to travel sprang from his interest in historical and literary associations.[4] To take this one step further, those historical and literary associations were the context of intimately personal verses. In the last analysis, the heart of Bashō's haiku is the very foundation of human perception of things—mind itself.

Operating superficially, the mind is random in its activity

and stale in its insights and images. With practice and experience, however, it is recognized as the empty infinity of the universe and of the self. The person who has become empty infinity and has integrated this experience of emancipation into everyday life finds expression in words and actions that are identifiable in spirit and character. Here lies my conviction that Bashō's haiku are to be read from the fundamental standpoint of Zen. He wrote of dusty roads, bird songs, and cool breezes; of ideas, emotions, and recollections; of folklore, ancient poetry, and Japanese history—playing with these forms and their words in a way that resonates deepest experience. My task is to make that way clear, to compare it with the way expressed in excerpts from Zen literature, and to open the door to Zen in the process.

Although I do not intend this book to be a contribution to literary history or criticism, one should begin any study of Bashō with at least a brief biography and an outline of his literary heritage. For more complete accounts, especially a presentation of Bashō's development as a poet, see Makoto Ueda's *Matsuo Bashō*.[5]

Bashō's Life Matsuo Kinsaku, later to take the name Bashō, was born in 1644 to a samurai family that was in the service of the lord of Ueno in the town of Iga, near Kyoto. This was in the early part of the Tokugawa period (1603–1868), and his birth roughly coincided with the closing of Japan to foreigners. This drastic policy of self-imposed seclusion caused Japan to turn in upon itself, seeking its own resources, and one result of this was a remarkable cultural efflorescence beginning in the second half of the seventeenth century. Bashō and the humanist poet Saikaku (1642–93) were nearly exact contemporaries, squarely in the vanguard of this explosion of creative activity, and Chikamatsu (1653–1724), the great dramatist of the puppet theater of Osaka, flourished only slightly later. *Ukiyo-e* ("pictures of the floating world"—the well-known paintings and woodblock prints) developed during this time, and ethics, history, jurisprudence, and other cultural forms reached maturity.

As a boy, Bashō was a page at Ueno Castle and a companion of the young lord, a lad about his age. The two youths were both interested in poetry, and they encouraged and influenced each other in this until the untimely death of the young lord, when Bashō was in his early twenties. This tragedy brought an important change to Bashō's life: he retired from service at the castle, perhaps because in his grief he found a deeper commitment to the way of poetry and felt his responsibility to the castle family was to some degree relieved. In any case, he seems to have spent time during the subsequent years of his youth studying with distinguished teachers of literature in Kyoto.

When he was about twenty-eight, Bashō moved to Edo, again for reasons that are not completely clear. After a struggle to support himself, he became at length established as an independent master of haiku. A wealthy merchant gave him a cottage that was surrounded by banana trees and known as *Bashō An* (Banana Tree Hermitage), and Bashō came to be known by the name of his house.

During his thirties, Bashō's poetry developed from mere cleverness through poignant self-doubt and self-search. With his model haiku "The Old Pond," written when he was forty-two, he seemed to come into his own as a mature poet, and his haiku that bear true Zen import date from this time.

Bashō wandered on pilgrimages during the last ten years of his life, sometimes alone, but often with one or two companions, visiting famous places and meeting with fellow poets and disciples. He died on such a pilgrimage at the age of fifty.[6]

The Development and Form of the Haiku   Historically, haiku developed from *renku,* the linked verse form that was popular among leisure classes in Japan from the earliest literate times. One poet would write a line of seventeen syllables, and another would cap that with a line of fourteen syllables. A third poet would add another line of seventeen syllables that would be linked to the first two lines in poetical intention. A fourth poet would cap that, and so on. The result would be a long poem of verses linked with associations shared by the participants, and the movement in imagery, intention, and implication would, when successful, be fulfilling for the entire party. Bashō himself participated in many such sessions with his students and friends, and these formed an important part of his life as a poet.[7]

In the middle of the fifteenth century, two hundred years before Bashō was born, people began writing the *hokku,* the opening line of the linked poem, as a separate form. Thus developed the shortest verse form in the world, just one line of seventeen syllables, now called haiku. The earlier name hokku means literally "verse that presents" or "verse that breaks out," indicating its function as the initiating verse of the long linked poem. Its development as an independent form is clearly a shift in poetic intent from interplay of cultural and literary associations to the more intimate task of presenting the vital experience of the thing itself. This was a development toward Zen, which emphasizes the full and complete presentation of the whole, with no burden of associational meaning whatever.[8]

Haiku in English and the Form of This Book   In its classical form, the Japanese haiku is written as a single line of three units, five syllables in the first unit, seven in the second, and five again in the third. These segments of the original haiku are generally rendered as separate lines in translations of haiku into Western languages, giving foreign readers a rather distorted impression of the original poems. However, an attempt to be faithful to the Japanese form might create problems of comprehension in English, so I use the customary three lines in my literary versions, in the Romanized Japanese, and in the word-for-word translations. Most of the translations of haiku are my own, taken from Japanese references, usually *Bashō Kōza*

(Lectures on Bashō).[9] I do not cramp my translations by forcing conformity to a particular count of syllables.

The translations are followed by remarks on the form of the specific haiku and an interpretation of its idioms. Then comes my comment on the content of the haiku, and finally another verse, usually my own and not a haiku, intended as a further comment.

A Zen Wave

ONE

The Old Pond

The old pond;
A frog jumps in—
The sound of the water.

Furu ike ya   Old pond!
kawazu tobikomu   frog jumps in
mizu no oto   water of sound

THE FORM   *Ya* is a cutting word that separates and yet joins the expressions before and after. It is punctuation that marks a transition—a particle of anticipation.

Though there is a pause in meaning at the end of the first segment, the next two parts have no pause between them. In the original, the words of the second and third parts build steadily to the final word *oto*. This has penetrating impact—"the frog jumps in water's sound." Haiku poets commonly play with their base of three parts, running the meaning past the end of one segment into the next, playing with their form, as all artists do variations on the form they are working with. Actually, the word *haiku* means "play verse."

The Japanese language uses postpositions rather than prepositions, so phrases like the last segment of this haiku should be reversed when translated into English: "water of sound" becomes "sound of water."

COMMENT This is probably the most famous poem in Japan, and after three hundred years of repetition it has, understandably, become a little stale for Japanese people. Thus as English readers, we may have something of an edge in any effort to see it freshly.

The first line is simply "The old pond." This sets the scene —a large, perhaps overgrown lily pond in a garden somewhere. We may imagine that the edges are quite mossy and probably rather broken down. With the frog as our cue, we guess that it is twilight in late spring.

This setting of time and place needs to be established, but there is more. "Old" is a cue word of another sort. For a poet such as Bashō, an evening beside a mossy pond is ancient indeed. Bashō presents his own mind as this timeless, endless pond, serene and potent—a condition familiar to mature Zen students.

In one of his first *teishō* (presentations of the Dharma) in Hawaii, Yamada Kōun Rōshi said: "When your consciousness has become ripe by true zazen—pure like clear water, like a serene mountain lake, not moved by any wind—then anything may serve as a medium for enlightenment."[1]

D. T. Suzuki once said that the condition of the Buddha's mind while he was sitting under the bodhi tree was that of *sāgara mudrā samādhi* (ocean-seal absorption).[2] In this instance, "mudrā" is translated as "seal," as in "notary seal." We seal our zazen with our zazen mudrā, left hand over the right, thumbs touching. Our minds are sealed with the serenity and depth of the great ocean in true zazen.

It was in such a condition that the Buddha happened to look up and notice the morning star. As Yamada Rōshi has said, any stimulus would do—a sudden breeze with the dawn, the first twittering of birds, the appearance of the sun itself. It just happened to be a star in this case.

In Bashō's haiku, a frog appears. To Japanese of sensitivity, frogs are dear little creatures, and Westerners may at least appreciate this animal's energy and immediacy. *Plop!*

"Plop" is onomatopoeic, as is *oto* in this instance. Onomatopoeia is the presentation of an action by its sound, or at least that is its definition in literary criticism. The poet may prefer to say that he himself becomes that sound. Thus the parody by Sengai Gibon is very instructive:

> The old pond!
> Bashō jumps in,
> The sound of the water![3]

Hsiang-yen Chih-hsien became a sound while cleaning the grave of Nan-yang Hui-chung. His broom caught a little stone which sailed through the air and hit a stalk of bamboo. *Tock!* He had been working on the koan "My original face before my parents were born," and with that sound his body and mind fell away completely. There was only that tock. Of course, Hsiang-yen was ready for this experience. He was deep in the samādhi of sweeping leaves and twigs from the grave of an old master, just as Bashō is lost in the samādhi of an old pond, and just as the Buddha was deep in the samādhi of the great ocean.

Samādhi means "absorption," but fundamentally it is unity with the whole universe. When you devote yourself to what you are doing, moment by moment—to your koan when on your cushion in zazen, to your work, study, conversation, or whatever in daily life—that is samādhi. Do not suppose that samādhi is exclusively Zen Buddhist. Everything and everybody are in samādhi, even bugs, even people in mental hospitals. Absorption is not the final step in the way of the Buddha. Hsiang-yen changed with that tock. When he heard that tiny sound, he began a new life. He found himself at last, and could then greet his master confidently and lay a career of teaching whose effect is still felt today. After this experience, he wrote:

> One stroke has made me forget all my previous
>   knowledge.
> No artificial discipline is at all needed;
>   In every movement I uphold the ancient way
>   And never fall into the rut of mere quietism;
> Wherever I walk no traces are left,
>   And my senses are not fettered by rules of
>   conduct;
> Everywhere those who have attained to the truth
>   All declare this to be of the highest order.[4]

The Buddha changed with noticing the morning star—"Now when I view all beings everywhere," he said, "I see that each of them possesses the wisdom and virtue of the Buddha . . . "[5]—and after a week or so he rose from beneath the tree and began his lifetime of pilgrimage and teaching.

Similarly, Bashō changed with that *plop*. The some 650 haiku that he wrote during his remaining eight years point surely and boldly to the fact of essential nature. A before-and-after comparison may be illustrative of this change. For example, let us examine his much-admired "Crow on a Withered Branch."

> On a withered branch
> A crow is perched:
> An autumn evening.

Kare eda ni	Withered branch on
karasu no tomari keri	crow of perched:
aki no kure	autumn of evening

Unlike English, Japanese allows use of the past participle (or its equivalent) as a kind of noun, so in this haiku we have the "perchedness" of the crow, an effect that cannot really be duplicated in English.

Bashō wrote this haiku six years before he composed "The Old Pond," and some scholars assign to it the milestone position that is more commonly given the later poem.[6] I think, however, that on looking into the heart of "Crow on a Withered Branch" we may see a certain immaturity. Though the poem certainly demonstrates his evocative power, that is not enough. Something is missing. What this haiku shows us, in fact, is quietism, the trap Hsiang-yen and all other great teachers of Zen warn us to avoid. *Sāgara mudrā samādhi* is not adequate; remaining indefinitely under the bodhi tree will not do; to muse without emerging is to be unfulfilled.

Ch'ang-sha Ching-ts'en made reference to this incompleteness in his criticism of a brother monk who was lost in quietism:

You who sit on the top of a hundred-foot pole,
Although you have entered the way, it is not yet genuine.
Take a step from the top of the pole
And show your whole body in the ten directions.[7]

The student of Zen who is stuck in the vast, serene condition of nondiscrimination must take another step to become mature.

Bashō's haiku about the crow would be an expression of the "first principle," essential nature, emptiness all by itself—separated from the world of sights and sounds, coming and going. This is the ageless pond without the frog. It was another six years before Bashō took that one step from the top of the pole into the dynamic world of reality, where frogs play freely in the pond and thoughts play freely in the mind.

The old pond has no walls;
A frog just jumps in;
Do you say there is an echo?

29

TWO

The Mountain Path

In plum-flower scent
Pop! the sun appears—
The mountain path.

Ume ga ka ni	Plum of scent in
notto hi no deru	pop sun of appearance
yama ji kana	mountain path!

THE FORM   The single word *ume* refers to plum flowers. In English, the word "plum" refers to the fruit, and we must use two words to speak of the flowers. In Japanese or Chinese, it is quite the other way around. One must use at least two words to speak of the fruit. *Ga* indicates a tightly linked expression— "plum-flower scent." *Ni* (in) establishes the aroma of plum flowers as the environment of the entire poem.

The second segment of the poem uses the onomatopoeic *notto* to express the popping up of the sun. *Hi no deru* (the sun's appearance), following immediately thereafter, is in apposition to *notto*. Apposition has common usage in such phrases as "my brother the musician," and it is the same here, though one might miss it at first: Pop! the sun's appearance.

This second segment modifies the third, so that one might discursively translate the two together: "The mountain path as the sun comes popping up." But the *kana* at the very end of the verse is a cutting word that serves to emphasize the poem's final noun. As in "The Old Pond," the momentum here builds steadily to the end: "mountain path" is the ultimate subject of the poem.

COMMENT   This poem is dated 1694, the year Bashō died. It shows him as usual on pilgrimage—up before dawn, picking his way along a mountain path in the dim light. On the slopes of the mountain, groves of plum trees are in fragrant blossom, and this is a seasonal cue for the earliest spring—it is bitterly cold. Sometimes plum trees hold snow as well as flowers.

The scent of plum flowers in the cold of early spring has been a favorite of Japanese and Chinese poets from ancient times. It is also a model for emergence to realization from the difficult passage that necessarily precedes it—the valley of the shadow of death. In the *Eihei Kōroku* (All-Inclusive Records of Eihei Dōgen), Dōgen Kigen asks: "Without bitterest cold that penetrates to the very bone, how can plum blossoms send forth their fragrance all over the universe?"[1] Bashō is trudging along in the freezing, early morning, lost in the pervading scent of plum blossoms, ready at last in the depths of his psyche for the sun, and *notto,* it appears. *Pop,* he realizes it.

Notto. The Japanese language is full of onomatopoeia, and this fact relates deeply to the intimate (rather than abstract) nature of Japanese expression. English and American usage of onomatopoeia is largely restricted to representation of sounds, as in "bang-bang." But in Japan, emotions and completely silent external activities are also frequently expressed in this way. The photographer will say "*Niko-niko,*" an onomatopoeic evocation of the act of smiling, the inner expression of the sparkle of teeth and the feeling of delight. Children employ more onomatopoeia than adults, but adults in Japan commonly use the equivalent of "clop-clop," "grr-woof," and the like.

However, the expression *notto* is rather rare. My Japanese-English dictionary cites only this poem, using R. H. Blyth's translation, "on a sudden, the rising sun!" as an example.[2] Professor Blyth translated the term "suddenly" in another rendering of the haiku.[3] But "on a sudden" and "suddenly" are both descriptive terms. *Notto* and "pop" are the action itself—from the inside. Bashō's experience of nature was more than observation, more than commingling: the sun, as Bashō, went *notto.*

Professor Blyth's discursive translations do point up one very significant aspect of Bashō's expression: the immediacy implicit in *notto.* Yamada Kōun Rōshi often says that true realization will invariably be sudden—shallow, perhaps; slight, perhaps; but never gradual. With that *notto,* Bashō emerged from utter absorption in plum-flower scent into the world of path, pack, and staff.

Zen practice follows the same pattern, through concentration, realization, and personalization.* These are the three fundamental Ox-Herding Pictures, one might say, and none of us can afford to stop short of the third step.[4] We can see quite clearly Bashō's experience of all three in this haiku: first he is lost in fragrance only; then he pops up as the sun; and finally he pushes along in his personalization of the way. "The Old Pond" built simply toward the experience of *oto,* from samādhi to realization, but nothing of their application is even implied in the poem itself. In this latter haiku, however, the

---

* English terms of Yamada Rōshi.

Wooden image of Bashō, Tokugawa period, provenance unknown. Collection of Nakagawa Sōen Rōshi, on loan to the Maui Zendo. Dress is that of a Zen monk.

Yamada Kōun Rōshi after sesshin at the Maui Zendo. . . . . "When your consciousness has become ripe by true zazen—pure like clear water, like a serene mountain lake, not moved by any wind—then anything may serve as a medium of enlightenment." *(See page 26)*

movement builds through a sudden experience to personal integration of that experience and the world of coming and going. Concentration permits realization, but to reach maturity, one must take another step.

When Hakuin Ekaku was very old, he had a marvelous reputation all over Japan, and hundreds of students came to study with him. But he had just a little house for a temple. To this day, that temple has no separate zendō (meditation hall), and by no means could all of the monks crowd into the temple, so some sat in the graveyard, and some found space under pine trees on the beach nearby. Hakuin, then in his middle eighties, tottered amongst these students, weeping because he no longer had the strength to urge them on with his stick. This was Hakuin's personalization of the way.[5]

What about the Priest Chu-chih? Whenever he was asked a Dharma question, he would hold up one finger. When he was about to die, he said to his assembled monks: "I received this one-finger Zen from T'ien-lung. I've used it all my life, but have not exhausted it." Having said this, he entered Nirvana.[6] This was Chu-chih's personalization of the way.

Chu-chih practiced zazen very rigorously before he met Hang-chou T'ien-lung. T'ien-lung held up a finger and Chu-chih abruptly saw it in the context of vast, empty reaches of countless universes. Seeing one finger, hearing a frog jump into the water, experiencing the sunrise, washing one's face in the early morning—anything will serve as a medium of enlightenment if the mind is serene and clear through earnest zazen.

For the rest of his life, Chu-chih embodied the tao (way) of the Buddha and of all succeeding Buddhist teachers down to his own master. Whenever he was asked about the Buddha Dharma, he always held up one finger. True maturity.

Bashō embodied the tao, hiking through the mountains and writing haiku. Chu-chih presented the same true nature, with one finger, as did Hakuin, lost in his tears. One stands up, sits down. The great way is none other than that.

Appearing completely—
The sun and plum flowers,
Bashō, you, and I.

THREE

Autumn in Kiso

Now being seen off
Now seeing off—the outcome:
Autumn in Kiso.

Okuraretsu	Being seen off now
okuritsu hate wa	seeing off now upshot:
Kiso no aki	Kiso of autumn

THE FORM   This poem hinges on the words *hate wa* (the outcome) at the end of the second line. The passive "Now being seen off," and the active, "Now seeing off," form a nominative phrase with "outcome." Our clue to realize this is the particle *wa*, which indicates that the preceding is the subject. So the poem may be rendered more discursively: "As to the outcome of now being seen off and now seeing off: autumn in Kiso."

COMMENT   I have found only three translations of this poem
into English, one each by R. H. Blyth, Donald Keene, and
Nobuyuki Yuasa. All three miss the essential point, the essential hinge of *hate wa,* "the outcome." Professor Blyth omits
it completely in his version:

> Seeing people off,
> Being seen off,—
> Autumn in Kiso.[1]

Professor Keene renders the expression as "journey's end":

> So often seen off,
> So often parting, journey's end—
> Autumn in Kiso.[2]

I puzzled over this latter version, rejecting it at last. The
implication that the journey's end is the autumn in Kiso places
too heavy an existential weight on the autumn of Kiso as a kind
of ultimate resting place. Such a meaning does not seem coher-
ently linked with "So often seen off, / So often parting,
. . ." Furthermore, the word "journey" does not appear in
the original, and the context of the poem was Bashō, midway on
his pilgrimage to see the full moon at Sarashina, bidding farewell to his friends. Professor Yuasa strays even further:

> Bidding farewell,
> Bidden goodbye,
> I walked into
> The autumn of Kiso.[3]

Farewells are an important point in human relationships.
Friendship is mutual investment, and the time of farewell is
the time of assurance of that investment. Our love remains
with you; our love goes with you. This is the content of being
seen off and of seeing off.

38

People in the West, sometimes quite insensitive to the importance of farewells, can learn from the Japanese, who say farewell to the very end. They wave and wave until their friends are out of sight. One meaning of *hate* is "extremity," and perhaps one interpretation of the poem could be waving and being waved at until there is nothing left but the autumn of Kiso. Such a meaning would be a little satirical, rather out of keeping with Bashō's spirit. I think we can go deeper.

The ending *(tsu)* of the verbs in the first two segments of this haiku means "now," in the sense "now you see it; now you don't." The sequence "Now being seen off; / now seeing off" is made especially poignant by the fact that this was Bashō's second farewell, in a period of just a few months, to his friends at Gifu.

Now our friends say farewell to us; now we say farewell. What is the outcome? Now on the Kiso road at Gifu, now at Honolulu Airport, now at Maui Memorial Hospital. Now we receive a lei, now we give a lei; now we are wept for, now we weep for. What is the upshot, after all?

In the "Song of Zazen" we recite: "Going and coming, never astray."[4] "Going and coming" would not be exactly the same as saying goodbye and being said goodbye to, but it, too, is a clear statement of the transitory nature of our lives. "Never astray"—is this not Bashō's intention? "God's in his heaven— / All's right with the world": Now being seen off, now seeing off—what is the outcome? Autumn in Kiso.

"God's in his heaven— / All's right with the world" means "this very place is the lotus land."[5] The wording and cosmology are not the same; Browning is not Hakuin, and Bashō is not you or I. But if the experience of coming and going, of farewells is true, then the outcome is all right.

When Hakuin wrote: "This very place is the lotus land," he was saying that everything is all right. The lotus land is a key point in Buddhism, and not all Buddhists agree that it is right here. For Pure Land Buddhists it is somewhere else. They long for it and appeal to the great mercy of Amitābha Buddha to draw them there. To this end, they devoutly recite his name *"Namu Amida Butsu—Nam man dam bu, nam man dam bu, nam man dam bu,"* and thus are assured of rebirth in the lotus land when they die. So the outcome for the Pure Land Buddhist differs somewhat from that of Hakuin, Browning, and Bashō. For one thing, it involves time.

Kobayashi Issa (1763–1827), one of the four outstanding haiku poets of Japan, inclined toward Jōdō Shin Buddhism, the greatest of the Pure Land movements. When his little daughter died, he wrote:

> While the dewdrop world
> Is the dewdrop world,
> Yet—yet—[6]

Tsuyu no yo wa	Dewdrop of world:
tsuyu no yo nagara	dewdrop of world while
sarinagara	however

This is a beautiful expression of the Jōdō Shin position: it is a sad world. As the *Diamond Sutra* says, all things are like a dream, a bubble, a fantasy, a dewdrop, a flash of lightning.[7] We come and go, being seen off and seeing off. This is the teaching of all the founders of all streams of Buddhism, and indeed of all streams of true religion. From ordinary observation, too, we know this to be true. In our hearts we long for the great mercy of Amitābha, who will draw us from this life of farewells to the lotus land, where we may find peace. *"Namu Amida Butsu—nam man dam bu, nam man dam bu, nam man dam bu . . ."*

Issa's "yet—yet—" is *Namu Amida Butsu.* It is the cord attached to the figure of Amitābha that will draw the dying person to ease of heart. We find this same "yet—yet—" in *senryū,* the so-called satirical verses of Japan, in which there is earnest longing and gentle mockery of the human condition:

Is it forever?
Dancing girls
Are nineteen years old.

Itsumade ka	How long?
jūku jūku no	nineteen nineteen of
shirabyōshi	white dancers

Is this the unchanging matter? Is change the ultimate fact? The English word "ephemeral" comes from the name of a fly that lives only a few days at most. Dancing girls, too, soon are gone, but other dancing girls replace them, always nineteen. Is this the upshot, after all? We sense longing through the satire, humanity in the mockery.

In preparing this chapter, I remembered this senryū from my reading as a youth. It is cited in Asataro Miyamori's *An Anthology of Haiku: Ancient and Modern*, the first book of Japanese poetry that I read. But I remembered it as an example of cynicism, for Professor Miyamori translates it: "Forever, dancing girls / Are nineteen years of age."[8]

Just as Blyth and Keene missed the significance of *hate wa,* "the outcome," so Miyamori missed the point of *itsumade ka* —literally, "until when?" The anonymous author of this senryū is asking a question as an exclamation: "Is this the way it has to be? Is change the only reality? Save me from this apprehension. *Namu Amida Butsu.*" Scholar and lecturer to the emperor, Miyamori missed the note of dread and brought the poem forth as a cynical look at our human ways. Instead of the religious spirit that was implicit in the original, he gives us a reduced picture of people as thoughtless creatures, grasshoppers who sing away the summer. This reductionist attitude is the way to misery, and ultimately to fear.

With *Namu Amida Butsu,* the Pure Land believer finds assurance. With "Autumn in Kiso," Bashō expressed his assurance. One is the assurance of the future. The other is assurance of the present. Now being seen off; now seeing off—what is the upshot? Autumn in Kiso, rain in Manoa Valley, a gecko at the Maui Zendo—*chi chi chichichi.*

Paul Gauguin asked: "Where do we come from? What are we? Where are we going?" You will find these words inscribed in French in the corner of one of his greatest paintings, a wide prospect of Tahiti, children, young people, adults, old people, birds, animals, trees, and a strange idol. What is the upshot after all? Gauguin painted it very beautifully.[9]

Finding ease of heart in prayer, acknowledging ease of heart in daily affairs—these are the ways of religion and poetry. The way of prayer is clearly set forth for us. *Namu Amida Butsu.* Lord Jesus have mercy on me, a sinner.

What is the way of acknowledging ease of heart in daily affairs? It is just that autumn in Kiso. It is just that rain. It is just the gecko. We blink and miss the key word. It is just one, just two, just three, and so on as we count our breaths. Nothing is missing, nothing is left over.

"Yet—yet—" is also the point. *Namu Amida Butsu* is also the point. That too is assurance of the present in daily affairs. There is just "yet—yet—"

Please stop at that point. Enter that point. Someone asked me how long it would take to attain *kenshō,* realization experience. I answered: "No time at all."

What is the upshot after all? *Chi chi chichichi.*

> Sesshin passes
> Bell by bell—
> What is the end?

FOUR

Wisteria Flowers

When worn out
And seeking an inn:
Wisteria flowers!

Kutabirete	Worn out
yado karu koro ya	inn seek when!
fuji no hana	wisteria of flowers

THE FORM The verb phrase *kutabirete* . . . *karu* may be translated literally as "exhausting seek," where in the inevitably looser English construction we would say, "exhausted and seeking." The *ya* has some cutting-word implication, but more important, it joins with *koro* in a phrase meaning "just at the moment of." Discursively, the haiku could be translated; "Just when I was completely exhausted, searching for an inn, I came upon wisteria flowers."

COMMENT   Bashō traveled on foot, of course, often in rather poor health. The context of the verse in his journal reads: "Most of the things I had brought for my journey turned out to be impediments, and I had thrown them away. However, I still carried my paper robe, my straw raincoat, inkstone, brush, paper, lunch box, and other things on my back—quite a load for me. More and more my legs grew weaker and my body lost strength. Making wretched progress, with knees trembling, I carried on as best I could, but I was utterly weary."[1]

I recall again Dōgen's question: "Without bitterest cold that penetrates to the very bone, how can plum blossoms send forth their fragrance all over the universe?"[2] At the very point of despair, Bashō encounters the rich lavender wisteria flowers. We know from our own practice and from our reading in the psychology of religion that suffering precedes personal liberation, and knowledge of this offers some comfort in the difficulties of work on the first koan. R. H. Blyth said to me in one of our first conversations: "There is no satori without tears."

Indeed, Bashō seemed to seek such suffering. He once wrote:

> I am resolved
> To bleach on the moors;
> My body is pierced by the wind.

Nozarashi wo	Moor-bleached
kokoro ni kaze no	mind of wind of
shimu mi kana	pierce body!

Examining this determination to die on pilgrimage (which he actually did at last) together with the haiku on wisteria flowers, we can understand even better why it was that Bashō did not write about the famous moonlit scene of Sarashina rice fields that he made a pilgrimage to see. Not only was he concerned about the expression of essential nature through ordinary configurations, but these expressions seemed to well up in his practice of enduring to the limit. He was not sightseeing.

Sometimes it was the suffering itself that found expression:

> Fleas, lice,
> A horse pissing
> By my bed.

Nomi shirami	Fleas lice
uma no nyō suru	horse of pissing
makuramoto	bedside

Here Bashō was on his best-known pilgrimage—recorded in *Oku no Hosomichi* (The Narrow Way Within)*—at the northernmost turn of his travels. In a mountainous region, about to pass the barrier between two provinces, he was obliged by bad weather to spend three days at the home of a barrier guard. He counted himself lucky to have any accommodation at all in such a remote place, but the comforts were meager.

Most translators of this haiku interpolate some feeling of disgust. Donald Keene, who usually can be trusted to translate dispassionately, renders the verse:

> Plagued by fleas and lice
> I hear a horse stalling—
> What a place to sleep![4]

That is not what Bashō said or meant at all, for he was using that suffering; he was not used by it. Not a single syllable in his original words reflects self-pity. It was just nip! ouch! pshhh!

* *Oku no* means innermost: within the country, within the self. (See note 3.)

45

How does one understand suffering? Our practice at the Koko An Zendo and the Maui Zendo is not easy. But if tears are the tears of sincere pain, they carry precious virtue. Self-pity sullies this virtue, and when self-pity is projected, we have needless dissension in the *sangha,* the fellowship. The virtue itself shines forth with incisive spirit that drives through the darkness. The pain itself is just that pain.

I think that Paolo Soleri would understand Bashō. In his essay "Relative Poverty and Frugality," he writes: "The intent of relative poverty is not to suffer and to do penance for the sins of man and specifically for the sins of avarice, gluttony and covetiveness. It is instead to glorify life through the lean, conscious exercise of one's energies in the face of odds which when understood cannot but show themselves as 'overwhelming.' It is at its best to 'perform the tragic sense of life itself,' well knowing that it is the only true sense and it is a sense of unfathomable depth. A sense full of seminal particles, a sense that can give reason and scope to sufferance. . . . To impersonate the tragic sense of life is not, one must be clear, a morose and bleak prospect. It is a conscious development of the self along a path . . . irksome with the unexpected, the will-breaker, the mystifier, the barbaric, the blasphemous, the malicious. . . ."[5]

Not to mention fleas. Bashō did not use the pilgrimage simply as a means. It was his best form of life. Out of that life emerged his experience of the wisteria flowers. Out of that life emerges expression of the peaks of life, the nips, the pain, the horse pissing. These are the seminal particles that give reason and scope, that give jewels of imperishable haiku:

> Ah, how glorious!
> Green leaves, young leaves
> Glittering in the sunlight.

Ara tōto	Ah glorious
aoba wakaba	green leaves young leaves
hi no hikari	sun of light

Hi no hikari, light of the sun, is a kind of pun, for the Japanese also pronounce the same ideographs as *Nikkō* when they try to approximate the Chinese reading of these ideographs. Nikkō is the name of a place, a tourist target in Bashō's day, as it is now. Famous for its natural beauty, it has been a Buddhist center since the eighth century. Its association with Kōbō Daishi (774–835), founder of the Shingon sect, and Jikaku Daishi (792–862), founder of the Tendai sect, was followed by imperial patronage and, finally, just before Bashō's time, Buddhist temples and Shinto shrines were erected there in memory of two great Tokugawa shoguns, Ieyasu (r. 1603–16) and Iemitsu (r. 1623–51). These later buildings are renowned for their elaborate design and decoration, the fullest expression of Japanese rococo. There is a saying in Japanese, "Don't say splendid [*kekkō*] until you have seen Nikkō."

Bashō didn't even say "Nikkō," though he went there. He was moved by the presences of Kōbō Daishi and Ieyasu, we may be sure. *Tōto* means "noble" in the highest sense. But it was the glory of the young leaves in the light of the sun that evoked his "Ah!" experience.

Nowadays there is a freeway to Nikkō, but in Bashō's time he and the other pilgrims had to climb there on foot. He mentions the arduous nature of the climb in his journal, and "Ah!" is the jewel in that setting, the sunlight in the pain of the climb.

We can see this pattern of pain and realization, or pain as realization, in virtually every Zen story. Yamada Kōun Rōshi says: "Pain in the legs is the taste of Zen."

Pai-chang Huai-hai and Ma-tzu Tao-i were taking a walk. Suddenly a wild duck flew up. Ma-tzu said: "What is that?"

Pai-chang said: "A wild duck."

[This reminds me of when I touch someone's knee in the *dokusan* room and ask: "What is that?" Most people can do as well as Pai-chang this far.]

Anyway, Ma-tzu said: "Where did it go?"

Pai-chang said: "It flew away." [This is like the usual reply: "That's my knee."]

Ma-tzu laid hold of Pai-chang's nose and gave it a sharp twist. Pai-chang cried out in pain. Ma-tzu said: "Why, it didn't fly away at all!"[6]

The point of this koan is not the progression from pain to realization, or pain as a reminder of realization. The simple twist of the nose would not bring kenshō to an ordinary person, any more than a fleabite would evoke a haiku. It is the lean, conscious exercise of one's energies in the face of profoundly difficult odds that may bring forth insight. Is that duck not right here? Why are you lying back and postponing that realization?

Bashō's poverty, like Thoreau's, was relative. He was burdened with necessary things, and could smile wryly at them. Nakagawa Sōen Rōshi once said to me: "You should carry your koan mu lightly." I did not know what he meant. I was burdened too heavily with my anxiety to resolve it. I could not appreciate mu for itself.[7] Use your pain; do not be used by it.

> In the kona storm
> Our *kahawai* rages
> And bufos sit deep in the mud.

In Hawaii, the wind blows violently from the south in a kona storm, rather than from the usual trade-wind direction. Near the Maui Zendo, the little stream, kahawai in Hawaiian, rolls boulders and uproots trees. Big toads show only their noses.

FIVE

Quail

Now, as soon as eyes
Of the hawk, too, darken,
Quail chirp.

Taka no me mo   Hawk of eyes too
ima ya kurenu to   now as-soon-as darken when
naku uzura   cry quail

THE FORM   Bashō used a number of postpositions and other particles to convey his meaning in this haiku. *No* means "of," while *mo* is "also" or "too." *Ya* carries its implication as a cutting word, but here also means "as soon as." *Nu*, as the ending of the verb *kurenu*, indicates "definitely," or "completed," and *to* means "when." "Eyes of the hawk too are darkened" means that everything has become dark. When the hawk can no longer see, the quail begin chirping in the bushes.

COMMENT   This verse reflects Bashō's sensitivity to the interplay of life in nature. The quail hides during the day in prudent respect for the hawk. The hawk preys upon quail, the quail upon insects, the insects upon smaller things. Yet each is pursuing its own life quite independently.

But this is only an overtone of the verse. More fundamentally, it points up the epoch of sunset, which, like sunrise, is a point of great change. It is not only the beauty of sun and clouds that affects us at such times. We and the world are transformed and become new. I am reminded of the first of T. S. Eliot's "Preludes:"

> The winter evening settles down
> With smell of steaks in passageways.
> Six o'clock.
> The burnt-out ends of smokey days.
> And now a gusty shower wraps
> The grimy scraps
> Of withered leaves about your feet
> And newspapers from vacant lots;
> The showers beat
> On broken blinds and chimney-pots,
> And at the corner of the street
> A lonely cab-horse steams and stamps.
>
> And then the lighting of the lamps.[1]

When I taught this poem in high school, one of my students wrote a paper on the continuation of day into night that is implied in the line, "And then the lighting of the lamps." The dreariness of the day in the London slum becomes the dreariness of evening. Yet there is still some magic remaining. Even today, the small child gets a thrill from turning on the electric light at evening. The day is past; the night begins. The light of the sun becomes that of the lamp. My boyhood visits to relatives who had no electricity were enhanced at evening when the kerosene lamps and candles were lit.

The late Yasutani Hakuun Rōshi giving teishō at the Zen Center of Los Angeles. . . . . "The compassion of the undifferentiated body of no cause, comes burning forth." *(See page 59)*

Detail of *Evening Rain*, by Bashō. . . . "I am resolved / To bleach on the moors; / My body is pierced by the wind." *(See page 107)*

Sitting in the dōjō and allowing it gradually to become dark before turning on the lights is an important device in our practice. Leaders in Rinzai-Zen monasteries make the most of it. At sunset, monks gather in the zendō while one of their brothers strikes the great temple bell outside to punctuate his reading of the *Kannongyō* (Avalokiteshvara Sūtra). As it gradually gets darker, they sit silently in zazen, and when the head monk can no longer discern the lines in the palm of his hand, he signals for *kinhin*, formal walking in line around the dōjō, which begins the evening program.

As the sun changes to the lamp, zazen changes to kinhin, the eyes of the hawk change to the chirping of the quail. Step by minute step, the universe changes. Now light, now dark, now hawk, now quail, now sea, now land. It is at the edge of transition that we find experience.

In Guam there is a fish that climbs trees—well, little bushes, anyway. When you walk near them, the fish scatter hurriedly and plunge back into their original element. These first amphibia, far older than the earliest human, yet still at the very point of transition from the sea, evoke the experience of immediacy at the hinge of evolution.

Dōgen expressed the virtue of transition in these words: "When you practice Zen upward, each step is equal in substance."[2] What is the substance of turning on the lamp? What is the substance of the first chirp of the quail? What is the substance of the fish crawling up the branch? In minutely subtle ways, there is transformation through time, space, and agent. With each koan, your practice changes, and as the penetrating vitality of the hawk becomes the contented chirping of quail, the substance of no-quality is felt anew.

Here is another of Bashō's haiku about change at evening:

> The temple bell fades
> And the scent of cherry blossoms rises
> In the evening.

> Kane kiete
> hana no ka wa tsuku
> yūbe kana

> Bell fades
> flower of scent: strikes
> evening!

The movement of this poem is carried by the verb *tsuku*, which means "strike" or "ring." The cherry blossoms ring their scent. *Kane* is "bell," but always "temple bell" when used alone. *Kane* and *tsuku* have (in this instance) the same phonetic element in their ideographs, providing an intimate link between hearing and scenting. Harold G. Henderson translates:

> As the bell tone fades
> blossom scents take up the ringing—
> evening shade.[3]

I think this fails as an English verse, but it is a valiant attempt to render Bashō's tightly laced intention.

It is sunset time, and as the sound of the temple bell fades with the light, cherry blossoms are sensed, and it is evening. Wu-men Hui-k'ai says you must hear with your eye.[4] Bashō is saying you must hear with your nose. But that is a bit off the main point of this poem. The sound of the bell rises in the scent of the cherry flowers in the mind of Bashō in his haiku in English in my words in your mind in your vows in your bows in your laughter with your friends.

"Step by step" is karma, the law of the universe. When you are truly stuck on mu, then you pass mu. When you pass mu, then you pass the source of mu. When you pass the source of mu, then you stop the sound of that distant temple bell. So it goes. So it remains.

> Drink earth and sunshine
> Deep tonight;
> A toast to new life past.

SIX

Suma in Summer

Though the moon is full
There seems an absence—
Suma in summer.

Tsuki wa aredo	Moon: though there is
rusu no yō nari	absence as-though is
Suma no natsu	Suma of summer

THE FORM   Grammatically, the interesting thing about this poem is the lack of a reference for the word *rusu* (absence). Who or what is absent? This question is resolved, if not directly answered, with a reading of another of Bashō's haiku on the subject, written at the same time:

Though I view the full moon
Something is missing!
Suma in summer.

Tsuki wo mite mo	Moon seeing though
mono tarawazu ya	something missing!
Suma no natsu	Suma of summer

COMMENT How is it that Bashō feels something is missing
or absent? On other occasions, he found complete delight
in moon viewing. Just a year earlier, he wrote:

The autumn moon!
I walked around the pond
All night long.

Meigetsu ya	Famed moon!
ike wo megurite	pond-circling
yo mo sugara	night even to the end

I do not think that the difference is in the seasons. Bashō
does not mean that the element missing at Suma is the addi-
tional beauty of the moon at autumn. No, on one occasion
Bashō found fulfillment in the full moon, on another occasion
he did not. When we understand these two occasions, we
understand more about poetry and more about the nature of
the mature life.

Under the full moon on a clear night in the country we have
a sense of majesty, of emptiness, of vacancy. There is nothing;
stars are gone and we are reminded of Bodhidharma's words:
"Vast emptiness, nothing holy"—that is, so vast that all such
words as "holy" are absurd and meaningless. Bodhidharma
said this in confrontation with the emperor of China. The emperor could not understand, and pressed him with the question:
"Who are you?"

Bodhidharma said: "I don't know."[1] There is the root of

56

personal reality. When Vimalakīrti was asked about non-duality, he remained silent.[2] That silence, called the "thundering silence of Vimalakīrti,"[3] and Bodhidharma's words express the same emptiness, the same vacancy that lies at the heart of Buddhism, and that is now being uncovered in physics and astronomy. As the *Heart Sutra* says: "Form is no other than emptiness; . . . Form is exactly emptiness."[4]

On the one hand, you may get the impression that emptiness is dehumanizing, and in one respect this may be correct, a point I will come to later. But for the moment, see how emancipating emptiness can be. There is nothing sticking to anything. We are free even of ourselves. "We and this food and our eating are vacant."*

In this connection there is an interesting story about a man who had kenshō in the old days, when we were still at the original Maui Zendo building. He and I were moving through the practice of clarifying and deepening his experience in dokusan, and one day I missed him in the dōjō. I went upstairs to his room and found him sitting casually on his bed. I asked him why he wasn't at zazen. He shook his head and said: "It's all empty."

Though I did not take time at that point to discuss it and simply asked him to come down anyway, I could appreciate his situation. He was like the Buddha, who sat for a week or so after his great realization, enjoying his insight into the suchness and emptiness of all beings and all things, just as Bashō wandered about the pond in the moonlight all night long. But then what happened? The Buddha thought of his five disciples, who had abandoned him in despair when they saw him accept a bowl of curds from a woman of low caste. He arose, sought them out in the city, and shared with them the "Four Noble Truths."

* Literally, "the three wheels are vacant"—the doer, the doing, and the deed. (See note 5.)

What was missing for the Buddha during that last week under the bodhi tree? His karma was missing. When there is only emptiness, there is no karma. The Buddha's karma, like yours and mine, is to save all beings—thus we find completion in our lives and fulfillment of the Dharma. The *Heart Sutra* also says: "Emptiness is no other than form. . . . Emptiness is exactly form."[6]

What was missing for Bashō there on the beach of Suma? Maybe I am being presumptuous in speaking for him, but I think he is saying that the full moon in the empty sky on an empty beach is not enough. Nirvana all alone by itself is not enough.

Compare all this emptiness with still another haiku by Bashō on the full moon:

> At our moon-viewing party
> There is no one
> With a beautiful face.

Tsukimi suru	Moon viewing
za ni utsukushiki	party at beautiful
kao mo nashi	face even none

What homely bastards we are, sitting here in the moonlight! This haiku is almost a senryū, and sets forth a humorous acceptance of the humanity of moon viewing. Compared with the coolness of the lonely poet wandering about the pond in the moonlight all night long, we find here a warmth, a love, a sangha that is missing from the earlier poem. Though all of Bashō's haiku I have cited in this chapter were written after his milestone verse "The Old Pond," it is interesting to notice that the haiku expressing simply the moonlight was written just a year later, when he was forty-three; the haiku expressing something missing in the moonlight was written when he was forty-four; and the one so expressive of delight in old companions was written when he was forty-seven. I don't want to belabor the point, and indeed Bashō wrote haiku about aloneness to the end of his life, but I think one does mature toward fellowship, toward the form, perception, ideas, volition, and mind of the sangha. Form is emptiness, but with more maturity, one realizes that emptiness is form. We must experience the full moon just in itself, but the application of that experience is found among true companions. Moreover, in keeping with the expression in the *Heart Sutra* that "form is exactly emptiness; / Emptiness exactly form," experience and application go together.

When Michael Kieran and I visited Gary Snyder in the Sierra foothills in December 1975, we talked of many things. One thing that sticks in my head is Gary's dictum: "the community as dōjō." While we were talking, members of the community, some of them coming in from long distances, were bathing in the Snyder sauna.

The community as dōjō is a personal ideal for those whose energies tend naturally toward helping professions, toward creative work that will give pleasure to others, or toward restoring vitality and productivity to the earth. It is a sangha ideal for all of us who are concerned about making our Koko An Zendo and our Maui Zendo better centers for Zen practice.

However, something is missing from the moonlight of purest practice if energy is turned exclusively inward for the protection and support of a single individual or group. In fact, such orientation is a violation of our realization. Gary Snyder's work is based in the mountains of San Juan Ridge, but his community includes us all.

Yasutani Hakuun Rōshi said: "The compassion of the un-differentiated body of no cause comes burning forth."[7] The undifferentiated body of no cause is Kanjizai Bosatsu, the Bodhisattva who sees clearly that form, perception, ideas, volition, and consciousness are empty moonlight. Compassion that comes burning forth is Kanzeon Bosatsu, the Bodhisattva who perceives clearly the sounds of suffering in the world, and who responds accordingly, perhaps to write of homely companions.

Kanjizai and Kanzeon are two Far Eastern figures that developed from Avalokiteshvara, the ancient deity of mercy. Please do not cling to their names. They are sitting there on your cushions, or chopping California grass. Our first vow is to save all beings,[8] and finding a modest channel to fulfill that vow in the garden of the community is a natural movement of a natural experience. Labeling it "Bodhisattva," "Bosatsu," or "compassionate" is to confine the Buddha to the cortex.

Gary Snyder said it:

> You be Bosatsu,
> I'll be the taxi-driver
> Driving you home.[9]

SEVEN

That

In the morning dew
Dirtied, cool,
A muddy melon.

Asatsuyu ni	Morning dew in
yogorete suzushi	dirty cool
uri no doro	melon of mud

THE FORM   A straightforward verse, but difficult to translate. *Yogorete suzushi* presents two adjectives in sequence. In English we would write "dirty, cool" or "dirty and cool," but Japanese adjectives have a verbal force. In sequence the final one retains an adjectival ending, while the one or ones preceding the last take a kind of present-participle ending, so that a pidgin translation of the words might be "dirtying cool." This kind of formation gives organic coherence to a series of adjectives that we cannot render in English.

COMMENT   This chapter is based upon the theme of Bashō's "Morning Dew" verse, but it was inspired by a recent poem of Joyce Carol Oates:

THAT

　　　　single pear in its ripeness
this morning swollen-ripe
its texture rough, rouged

　　　more demanding upon the eye than the tree
branching about it
more demanding than the ornate drooping limbs
of a hundred perfect trees

　　　yet flawed: marked as with a fingernail
a bird's jabbing beak
the bruise of rot
benign as a birthmark
a family blemish

　　　still, its solitary stubborn weight is a bugle
a summoning of brass
the pride of it subdues the orchard
more astonishing than the acres of trees
the army of ladders
the workers' stray shouts

　　　　that first pear's weight
exceeds the season's tonnage
costly beyond estimation
a prize, a riddle
a feast.[1]

It is clear that Joyce Carol Oates was on Bashō's wavelength. It is just *that!* That dirty, cool melon. That ripened, blemished pear.

It might be possible for the reader to pass over Bashō's presentation as simply the description of an object. Oates, however, works a lengthy comment into her poem. That pear, she says, is more demanding on the eye than the "ornate drooping limbs of a hundred perfect trees." It is just that pear in the whole universe. It is "a bugle / a summoning of brass." Attention! Infinitely precious, so valuable its cost cannot be estimated. This is just what Bashō presents with his cool melon—blemished in a benign way that enhances the experience, as Oates's pear is flawed to be altogether unique.

As a youth, I worked in a pear shed in Lake County, California, one of my first jobs. I had to keep the culls from backing up on the sorting belt. All day long I carried boxes of discards from the packers to the shipping platform; from there they were taken I knew not where, perhaps to the dump, perhaps to the pigs. But each of those pears was altogether unique, infinitely precious.

We think in terms of mass, utility, and generality. As the child grows up, his or her teeth are straightened to a certain norm. This may be necessary in some cases to provide a good bite, but what is more distinctive than a crooked tooth? It adds appeal to a face and to a smile. Teeth that protrude a little, a birthmark, an eye with a cast—now there is a unique individual.

With the flaw, with the blemish, with the mud, we see *that*. I think Oates knew very well whereof she spoke when she used "That" as a title.

The Sanskrit term *tathatā* (thusness or suchness) is a key word in Buddhism. It is related to a name for the Buddha—Tathāgata, meaning "the one who thus comes"—that is, the one whose appearance is just *that*. The Japanese translate tathatā as *shinnyō*, true likeness. In the Kegon Sect, this shinnyō is the word used to mean "phenomena," or "things."

Of course! Each phenomenon is *that*. Just that dirty melon. Just that flawed pear. Just that footfall in the hallway. Just that whiff of incense. If you are equal to *that,* the tiny blue flowers of *hona-hona* grass are like stars on a clear night.

So far as I can determine, R. H. Blyth is the only translator of the ''Morning Dew'' haiku. He tried three different versions, using the plural ''melons'' in two of them.[2] Of course, in Japanese there is a choice. Without context, you can't tell whether *uri* is one or a hundred-thousand melons. But the context here is the haiku itself. Singular is the most vivid.

Here is another *that:*

> The *matsutake!*
> A leaf from an unknown tree
> Stuck fast.

Matsutake ya	*Matsutake!*
shiranu ko no ha no	unknown tree of leaf of
hebaritsuku	stuck fast

Matsutake—literally, ear of the pine tree—is an edible fungus that grows from the bark of pine trees in Japanese forests.

There is slightly more association in this poem than in the one about the melon. We may suppose that Bashō has been given or has bought the matsutake for food. The human mind tends to separate food from its sources, so we can eat brains, tongues, and intestines without a qualm. But seeing the leaf from the unknown tree stuck fast to the matsutake puts Bashō in touch with the natural origins of that fungus in the forest, and with his own natural origins. Bashō recites with us our mealtime sutra: ''First, we consider in detail the merit of this food and remember how it came to us.''[3]

But deeper even than that, the matsutake, enhanced by the flaw of a stray leaf sticking to it, is just *that*. Everything else disappears. This is the fact of experience, and also the fact of practice. The koan mu must be like this. Key mu to your breaths, exhalation and inhalation, or exhalation only. Let there be only mu inside, only mu outside, only mu in the whole universe. Bring mu into sharp focus—vivid and clear. No gap between yourself and mu. You must become mu itself.[4]

With such a practice comes realization, not as straight-line cause and effect, but as a miracle.

A monk said to Tung-shan Shou-ch'u: "What is Buddha?" Tung-shan said: "*Ma san chin* [three pounds of flax]."[5]

Flax is not melon, Tung-shan is not Bashō, the koan is not the haiku, but the miracle is the same: "Three pounds of flax." Mu. *Crack!*

Simone Weil says: "Even if our efforts of attention seem for years to be producing no result, one day a light that is in exact proportion to them will flood the soul."[6] Here is that light:

> The cry of the cuckoo
> Goes slanting—ah!
> Across the water.[7]

Hototogisu	Cuckoo
Koe yokotō ya	voice slants!
mizu no ue	water of above

This is Professor Blyth's translation, and with its echo of Gerard Manley Hopkins, another poet who knew vividness, I cannot imagine a better English version.

The cry of the cuckoo slants—a brilliant image for its passage across the water of the lake. Just that sound out of nowhere. In nowhere. Total presentation.

Unless you walk hand in hand with Bashō, you cannot realize his mind. Here is a translation that misses the mark:

> A *hototogisu*
> Casts a thread of sound
> Over the water.[8]

"A thread of sound" changes the original too much. Vividness is gone. "Slants" disappears, and the poem becomes meaningless. But worse is to come. An American scholar translates it:

> As the cuckoo flies
> its singing stretches out
> upon the water lies.[9]

With a desire to rhyme and with a misunderstanding of the word *ue* (which means "surface," but also the area above the surface) the translator not only ruins the poem, he corrupts it. A clearcut experience is reduced to a mistaken, abstract description of something that did not and could not happen. How can singing stretch out and lie down?

But, as we used to say in my childhood in Honolulu, more worse yet! Look at this version:

> The voice of the hototogisu
> Dropped to the lake
> Where it lay floating
> On the surface.[10]

The poor thing. You laugh, but Bashō is running from the room, holding his stomach.

Doctor Johnson says: "Why Sir, Sherry is dull, naturally dull; but it must have taken him a great deal of pains to become what we now see him. Such an excess of stupidity, sir, is not in Nature."[11]

It is possible to train yourself to be dull. Do not pay attention to things. Preoccupy yourself with brooding. The dull person is one who has practiced not noticing closely. The fatuous person is one who hides from the vital animal, like the king in W. S. Merwin's story "The Fountain" who could not bring himself to acknowledge the animal that proved itself to be the genius of water in a time of drought. Not only could he not acknowledge it, he killed it, and thus destroyed himself, his sons, and his kingdom.[12]

This is the opposite of our way. When we practice mu closely in the dōjō or focus clearly on what we do when we are away from our cushions, there can only be concern for mu, concern for the things, animals, and people of our lives. Self-preoccupation drops away, and we are totally weightless. Then even serious disease need not be a source of worry.

The path of clarity is the path of weightlessness. There is only that cry slanting across the water, nothing else. There is not even a bird, only the cry. There is only the pear, rouged and flawed. There is only the matsutake with a strange leaf stuck to it. Assumptions, explanations (including this chapter), extrapolations, personal associations—all add weight, and the experience will not rise.

Dulled by this pale cast of thought, you stay in the dumps, speaking dumpily, behaving dumpily, doubting the airy world of poetry and religion. Once when I was teaching school, one of my students wrote an essay on the importance of looking at the sky. Most people, he said, do not look at the sky enough. Things outside yourself, even physical and mental qualities of yourself that you notice objectively—these touch off true, brilliant experience.

Yasutani Hakuun Rōshi wrote: "From morning to night, vividly, immediately, the original face of universality moves briskly in detailed particulars. Whenever, wherever, it is the full presentation—full presentation of absolute virtue. There we find no truth or delusion. It is the fact of original essence. Please savor this fully."[13]

What are the detailed particulars? The melon. The pear. The matsutake. Full presentations of absolute virtue. Nothing is missing. Nothing left over.

> Late in the night
> The full moon sets
> Banana leaves barely stir in the wind.

EIGHT

That's Interesting

A day when Fuji
Is obscured by misty rain!
That's interesting.

Kiri shigure	Mist rain
Fuji wo minu hi zo	Fuji can't see day!
Omoshiroki	interesting

THE FORM *Kiri shigure* is misty rain associated with the autumn season. The first segment sets the scene for Mount Fuji, and the postposition *wo* indicates that Fuji is the object of the verb phrase "can't see." *Zo* is a particle indicating strong emphasis for the preceding word, "day."

The third segment is just one word, *omoshiroki*. Pronounced *omoshiroi* in modern Japanese, this is probably among the fifty most common words in the language. It is used in many ways, to mean many things: interesting, entertaining, funny, jolly, odd, or favorable. It is even broader in implication than our word "funny." The usual meaning is, however, as I have translated—"interesting."

COMMENT   Mount Fuji is a miraculous mountain, even for Westerners. Set near the Pacific Ocean and rising for 12,000 feet, it is an almost-perfect cone. Sometimes on misty days, only a single line of one slope is visible, drawn endlessly, it seems, into the heavens. On clearer days, the mountain seems to hang high in the air like the Peak of Wonder, which is described in the *Avatamsaka Sūtra* as the center of paradise. In the crisp air of autumn it stands out boldly against the dark sky, and in winter it appears like a dream of white in a sky of palest blue.

In poems of earliest Japan, gathered in the *Man'yōshū* (Collection of Myriad Leaves, c. 760), the first anthology of Japanese literature, Mount Fuji is an object of worship:

> Lo, there towers the lofty peak of Fuji
> From between Kai and wave-washed Suruga.
> The clouds of heaven dare not cross it,
> Nor the birds of the air soar above it.
> The snows quench the burning fires,
> The fires consume the falling snow.
> It baffles the tongue, it cannot be named,
> It is a god mysterious.
> The lake called Se is embosomed in it,
> The river we cross, the Fuji, is its torrent,
> In the land of Yamato, the Land of the Rising Sun,
> It is our treasure, our tutelary god.
> It never tires our eyes to look up
> To the lofty peak of Fuji.[1]

Though dormant now, Mount Fuji was an active volcano when this was written; "the lake called Se" has since been divided into two by volcanic action. Of course, the idea that clouds dare not cross Fuji is a poetical conceit; sometimes it is closed in by clouds, as Bashō indicates. But by this conceit, we may share the awe that sensitive Japanese people feel about Fuji to this day.

In a land where all mountains are venerated, each having its own shrine at the summit, Mount Fuji is unquestionably the Olympus. Even today, for all the commercial preoccupations in modern Japanese culture, many hundreds—perhaps thousands—of people climb to the top every day in the summer, camping there overnight in crude inns in order that they may see the sunrise the next morning.

In old times, the day when Mount Fuji could not be seen by the traveler along the Tōkaidō road, which ran between Tokyo and Kyoto, was a deeply disappointing one. In modern times, people on the trains that run along the old Tōkaidō route may be found peering for the first glimpse of Fuji in clear weather, or watching intently in the right direction if the day is overcast. In the latter case, sometimes the clouds will lift momentarily, and there will be a chorus of "ahs" passing the whole length of the train.

Given a context of such universal admiration of Fuji, Bashō's haiku celebrating the day when the great mountain cannot be seen has posed a good deal of difficulty for scholars of Japanese literature. What could Bashō have meant? Some translate the key portion, "that day, too, is interesting," as though Bashō intended to imply a kind of equality of values—as though to say, "Fuji is good; no-Fuji is also good."[2]

But if Bashō had wished to convey the meaning of "too," he would have used that word. However, instead of mo (also), he used the emphatic zo. This zo isolates the subject of attention and its circumstances from everything else. Bashō says: "This very day, this Fuji-obscured day, is itself interesting."

Another tack translators have taken in their attempts to make sense of this haiku involves the interpolation of "although." "Although Fuji is obscured by misty rain, the day is interesting."[3] This, too, is highly destructive of the poem's intention, for it is not a verse of consolation for thwarted Fuji viewers: "Cheer up; maybe you can't see Fuji today, but there are other things that compensate for the loss." Not at all. Here again, Bashō would not have used *zo* to convey such a meaning. He was focused on that very day, saying that *that* day, with the particulars of misty rain and the impossibility of seeing Fuji, was itself interesting.

Perhaps you might be tempted to dismiss Bashō's true meaning as a Pollyanna view of life—everything *is* for the best in this best of all possible worlds, as Candide says. You might have a similar reaction to the koan "Every day is a good day:"

Yun-men Wen-yen addressed his assembly and said: "I do not ask you about the fifteenth of the month. How about after the fifteenth? Come, give me a verse about this."

Then, answering for the assembly, he said: "Every day is a good day."[4]

In his comment on this case, Yasutani Hakuun Rōshi observes that the full moon appears on the fifteenth of each month on the old Chinese lunar calendar. The completeness of the full moon may have reference to the Zen experience, he says. So Yun-men might be saying: "I do not ask about the day you experience satori. How about after that day?"[5]

"Every day is a good day." This response is not in the spirit of Pollyanna. It should not be taken superficially to blur distinctions—good when it shines, good when it rains. Yun-men was not a master to resort to saying "Nothing special," or to shouting *"Katsu!"* in response to every question.

Look again at the poem that ended chapter two:

> Appearing completely—
> The sun and plum flowers,
> Bashō, you, and I.

71

Now the sunshine, now the misty rain, now a snowy cone, now a faint, beautiful line running to the heavens. Or we may say, now sweet, now bland, now salty, now bitter.

We have a good, simple diet at our two centers, but is it a Zen diet? If the soup is bland, we add sesame salt or soy sauce, and we miss the point of bland soup. Bland soup has its own taste, and perhaps we should not be so quick to alter it.

When Nakagawa Sōen Rōshi accepts coffee and is offered cream and sugar to go with it, he says: "I'll have them in succession." So he drinks part of his cup black and then adds cream. He drinks a little more and then adds sugar. Now bitter, now creamy, now sweet. Each one is interesting. Each one is good.

Bashō wrote this haiku when he was forty years old, two years before "The Old Pond." It is moralistic—not basically, but in its overtone, I think. A little moralizing does not hurt, perhaps, especially when we restrain our strict, literalistic impulses and hold the lesson in perspective. Yamada Kōun Rōshi says the purpose of Zen is the perfection of character, and one fault of character is the tendency to hold fixed expectations. I expect my soup to be well salted. I expect my teacher to be severe. Here we are in Shizuoka Prefecture—I expect to see Mount Fuji.

Following former Lieutenant Hiroo Onoda's return to Japan in 1974 from his solitary thirty years as a World War II holdout on Lubang Island in the Philippines, he was asked on Japanese national television whether or not he had seen Mount Fuji as he flew over Japan on his return to Tokyo. He replied that he had not; the day was cloudy and he had been disappointed. Lieutenant Onoda must have had some inkling of Yunmen's mind—of Bashō's mind—to have sustained himself with only the barest essentials, day after day, for so many years. However, his application of that inkling related to his nation-state. Yun-men and Bashō had another application entirely.

We may find the equal of Yun-men and Bashō, however, in

many great personages, and the following is a story about one such fellow:

At the monastery of Fūgai Ekun, ceremonies delayed preparation of the noon meal one day, and the cook had to take up his sickle and hurriedly gather vegetables from the garden. In his haste, he lopped off part of a snake, but unaware that he had done so, he threw it into the soup pot with the vegetables.

At the meal, the monks thought they had never tasted such delicious soup, but the Master himself found something remarkable in his bowl. Summoning the cook, he held up the head of the snake, and demanded: "What is this?"

The cook took the morsel, saying: "Oh, thank you, Rōshi," and immediately ate it.

Senzaki Nyogen Sensei first told this story in English, and Paul Reps titled it "Eating the Blame."[6] The monk was not full of self-justification, sputtering in his anxiety to clear himself of blame in the eyes of the Rōshi: "Oh, it was late, er, and I, ah, had to hurry. . . ." By his free and self-assured action, that monk showed that he had no thought that the Master intended to accuse him of carelessness and cruelty. The Rōshi's challenge was a wonderful chance to show the virtue of a particular set of circumstances, and the cook was ready to meet that challenge, showing us with his response that there was nothing to carry over as blame. Surely Fūgai was pleased. That was a good day indeed.

> The morning mists rise
> And Fuji is revealed.
> Ah, the day is saved!

NINE

The Shepherd's Purse

When I look carefully—
Nazuna is blooming
Beneath the hedge.

Yoku mireba   Carefully looking-when
nazuna hana saku   *nazuna* flower blooms
kakine kana   hedge!

THE FORM   This is a unified haiku that builds toward the final cutting word, *kana*. The entire poem is an exclamation, but an exclamation mark in English would be too heavy. The *ba* ending of *mireba* indicates "if" or "when."

COMMENT   A rather ordinary-seeming verse, but one that is widely appreciated in Japan. The *nazuna*, a small plant called shepherd's purse in English, bears tiny white flowers with four petals. Even Bashō might be tempted to pass it by, but he does not. He is attracted by flecks of white beneath the hedge and pauses to look closely. There are nazuna flowers, blooming with full spirit.

Seeing the nazuna flowers evokes an "Ah!" of appreciation for the living things in themselves. Just those tiny flowers. In his essay "The Morning Glory," D. T. Suzuki comments on this verse: "Once off human standards which are valid only on the plane of relativity, the nazuna weeds match well with the peonies and roses, the dahlias and chrysanthemums. Bashō of course did not reason like this; he was a poet, and he intuited all this and simply stated: 'When closely seen, it is the nazuna plant blooming.' "[1]

Professor Suzuki then takes up the social implications of our inability to notice the nazuna: "We are always ready to destroy anything, including ourselves. We never hesitate to slaughter one another and give this reason: there is one ideology that is absolutely true, and anything and anybody, any group or any individual who opposes this particular ideology deserves total annihilation. We are blatantly given up to the demonstration of self-conceit, self-delusion, and unashamed arrogance. We do not seem nowadays to cherish any such feelings as inspired Bashō to notice the flowering nazuna plant. . . . We trample [such flowers] underfoot and feel no compunction whatever. Is religion no longer needed by modern man?"[2]

Quite an outburst from our kindly Sensei. One may feel that it is hardly upheld by the slight nature of the haiku—a quaint old Japanese poet gazing upon a weed three hundred years ago. Can we balance the peace movement, say, on such a delicate base? And how can Professor Suzuki justify bringing religion to the discussion?

I think it is possible to show how Bashō is teaching us religion with his nazuna haiku, and how the denial of the nazuna is "self-conceit, self-delusion, and unashamed arrogance." The first step in Bashō's teaching is to remove us from the "human standards which are valid only on the plane of relativity." These standards place peonies, roses, dahlias, and chrysanthemums on the level of beautiful flowers, and the nazuna on the level of weeds. When you're truly removed from that point of view, then unsalted food is unsalted, and salty food is salty—that's all. Then Koreans are Koreans; Japanese are Japanese—that's all. Neither can be ennobled; neither can be denigrated. Each can be enjoyed: the rose in the White House garden, the nazuna under the hedge. Projecting relative standards upon the nazuna is projecting conceit and arrogance. Only a weed! If we permit such a relative base of judgment to remain intact for the nazuna, then that same base will provide affection for Koreans and hatred for Japanese, or the reverse. We will be unable to see things, animals, and people as they are.

To continue on with Professor Suzuki: "When beauty is expressed in terms of Buddhism, it is a form of self-enjoyment of the suchness of things. Flowers are flowers, mountains are mountains, I sit here, you stand there, and the world goes from eternity to eternity; this is the suchness of things. A state of self-awareness here constitutes enlightenment, and a state of self-enjoyment here constitutes beauty."[3]

Upon seeing the flower, Bashō realized *this, this*. On seeing the flower, he enjoyed it. And on seeing the flower, he wrote the haiku. Professor Suzuki puts these three elements into philosophical categories as follows: "Enlightenment is the noetic aspect of *prajnā*-intuition, beauty is its affective aspect, and the great compassionate heart is its conative aspect. In this way we can probably understand what is meant by the doctrine of suchness."[4]

This remarkable passage sums up the unity of realization, aesthetic experience, and love. Noetic pertains to the mind, affective to emotion, and conative to desire or will. "Suchness" is such a dry word, and prajnā is only a sound from a dead language, but contained in them is this living trinity of experience: just that nazuna flower, just that beautiful nazuna flower, let me present you that nazuna flower. This is the trinity of seeing, appreciating, and sharing. True seeing is appreciating;

true appreciation is motivating. Thus the Buddha saw the morning star, enjoyed the morning star, and walked the length and breadth of India teaching his experience. These are the Three Bodies of the Buddha, the *Dharmakāya,* the *Sambhogakāya,* and the *Nirmānakāya*—the Body of Enlightenment, the Body of Bliss, and the Body of Manifestation.

Professor Suzuki's essay "The Morning Glory" is constructed around a haiku by Chiyo-ni, one of Japan's greatest poets:

> The well bucket
> Taken by the morning glory;
> I beg for water.[5]

Asagao ni	Morning glory by
tsurube torarete	well bucket taken
morai mizu	beg water

The poet came out for water in the early morning and found the morning-glory vine twined about the well bucket, so she was moved to beg water from the neighbors rather than to disturb the vine.

Some critics find this poem too precious, but Professor Suzuki points out that one of Chiyo-ni's variants for the version usually cited uses *ya* rather than *ni* at the end of the first segment. The *ya* serves to cut the verse at that point, and to express the "Ah!" experience of the poet, lost in just that morning glory. So Professor Suzuki translates the haiku:

> Oh, morning glory!
> The bucket taken captive,
> Water begged for.[6]

And he comments: "At the time, the poetess was not conscious of herself or of the morning glory standing against her. Her mind was filled with the flower, the whole world turned into the flower, she was the flower itself. When she regained

77

her consciousness, the only words she could utter were, 'Oh, morning glory,' in which all that she experienced found its vent.''[7]

This is the meaning of my words, "Enjoy your mu.'' Emerging from this enjoyment is the great compassionate heart, to beg for water rather than to disturb the vine. Emerging from this enjoyment we greet one another; we take care of each other's children; we resist inhumanity and injustice. Emerging from his appreciation of the nazuna haiku, Professor Suzuki berates the war psychology of nations and the self-centered arrogance of individuals.

I find that students who seek out the zendō as a sanctuary from social pressures may tend to object to the emphasis on compassion in Zen practice. I believe this reveals the self-centered nature of their original motive for doing zazen. Unless this self-concern is turned about, there can be no maturity.

Compassion takes practice, like any other kind of fulfillment. I am often told that compassion should flow naturally. This is true. Also, Mozart should flow naturally from your fingers when you sit at the piano. It is important and essential to understand that Zen is not *simply* a matter of spontaneity. It is also practice. By practicing zazen, you do zazen. By sitting with a half-smile, you practice enjoyment. By smiling at your friends, you practice the great compassionate heart. The act is the practice. The practice is the act. Sitting when you do not feel like it—that is zazen, that is the rare *udumbara* flower of Buddhahood. Smiling at your friends when you do not feel like it—that is compassion, annihilating greed, hatred, and folly, and giving life to the healing spirit of Kanzeon.

I have been told that practice of compassion is dishonest when one does not feel compassionate. This argument makes my blood boil. To what are you being honest? Nothing but a whim! You do not belong here.

If you say this is all didactic, I have no objection. The haiku master and the Zen master are teachers. Bashō's purpose was not merely self-expression. With his great compassionate heart, he was saying, "Go thou and do likewise." He even wrote some haiku that were didactic in content.[8] One such verse which fits our purposes neatly in this chapter is unfortunately only ascribed to Bashō:

> For one who says,
> "I am tired of children,"
> There are no flowers.

Ko ni aku to	"Children of tire"
mōsu hito ni wa	says person for:
hana mo nashi	flowers even none

This verse is titled "Shown to a Student," marking it as an occasional verse not originally composed for general education. *Hana* refers to cherry blossoms, and appreciation for the ephemeral beauty of cherry flowers marks a capacity to appreciate the best of human culture.

Bashō, or whoever wrote this verse, is saying that your realization, enjoyment, and love cannot be separated. When love is absent, cherry flowers go unappreciated, and the suchness of nazuna is unknown. Apparently the inspiration for this haiku is a poem in the *Man'yōshū* that warns there would be no memorial service for a mother who had a reluctant spirit in caring for her children.[9] The recreation of this idea by the haiku poet is deeper and more immediate than the original. There are no nazuna for such a parent. There is no realization of the Dharmakāya.

Ta-lung Chih-hung presents the final verse for us this time. A monk said to him: "The body of color perishes. What is the fixed Dharma body [*Dharmakāya*]?" Ta-lung said:

> The mountain flowers bloom like brocade;
> The river between the hills is blue as indigo.[10]

TEN

This Road

This road!
With no one going—
Autumn evening.

Kono michi ya	This road!
yuku hito nashi ni	goes person without in
aki no kure	autumn of evening

THE FORM Here again there is a cutting word at the end of
the first segment. The *ya* singles out the experience of "this
road," while linking it to the segments that follow. As in "The
Old Pond," the first segment expresses the mind of the poet
as well as his circumstances. *Ni* here means "in" or "in the
circumstances of."

COMMENT I should like to set forth comments about this

verse by other students of haiku before I enter my own. The editors of *Haikai and Haiku* say: "This poem is entitled 'A Reflection.' The lonely country road along which the poet is walking on an autumn evening appears to him to be a symbol of the path of poetry, which he must follow alone, if he is to realize his ideal."[1]

Michi (path or road) is written with the ideograph pronounced *tao* in classical Chinese, the *tao* of the *Tao Te Ching* (The Way and Power Classic; c. third century B.C.). *Michi* also means "way" or "-ism" in many Japanese idioms. *Haiku no michi* is "the way of haiku," the "*tao* of haiku," for example. You can see how the editors of *Haikai and Haiku* derived their interpretation. However, they permitted their associations to guide them without examining the primary intention of "This Road!" and thus they removed the poem from its immediate setting and limited it to secondary symbolism. I much prefer Makoto Ueda's suggestion that the road is both literal and symbolic, though I think perhaps he too is inclined to read excessive pessimism into Bashō's words.[2]

Asataro Miyamori translates the haiku:

> None goes along this way but I,
> This autumn eve.

He comments:

This was composed in September, 1694, Bashō's last year, at a tea house in the suburbs of Osaka. It was an autumn evening. In front of the tea house in question there lay a long highway, as far as the eye could reach. Along it not a soul was to be seen, except the poet himself. What a lonesome evening!

Such is the surface meaning, but the implied meaning is generally conjectured to be as follows:—The *haikai* world at large was dreary and lonesome like an autumn evening. The poet was afraid none of his pupils would be able to follow in his wake on the path of poetry.[3]

There are two possible conclusions to be drawn from these flaccid commentaries. The first is that the writers, despite their status as Japanese experts of haiku, had no eye for the *ya*, which points up the fundamental significance of the road itself. The second is that they were condescending to their Western readers.

In any case, both commentaries fail to touch the central point of the haiku. The editors of *Haikai and Haiku* assume Bashō is saying simply that he must strike out alone if he is to be a true poet. Miyamori acknowledges the lonely road as the "surface meaning" of the poem, but goes on to imply that the deeper meaning is symbolic: Bashō's disappointment with his disciples. These dubious conclusions follow naturally upon the original error of treating *michi* entirely as a secondary symbol instead of accepting it in the way Bashō showed he intended with his use of the cutting word *ya*: Ah, this road!

The fact is that Bashō enjoyed his students and took great interest in their work. In a section of his essays devoted to haiku poets of his time, his spirit of friendship and admiration is clearly set forth.[4]

More basically, any desire to go it alone and any feeling of disappointment in his students would be only the context of Bashō's experience. Quite the reverse of Miyamori's interpretation, the experience itself is central, clearly presented by the stark first segment and cutting word. It is this very road itself, with no people going along it. Yamada Kōun Rōshi often says: "When you stand up, there is only that standing up, with nothing sticking to it." "Just this! this!" is the "final phrase," said Yen-t'ou Ch'uan-huo.[5] Whatever the experience, if it is pure, there is nothing else in the whole universe.

"No one goes" is a reflection on "this road," anﬂ thus the title. "Nothing sticking to it" is a reflection on "just standing up." Reflection is musing upon experience for the poet or the Zen person. It is not brooding over other people's misunderstanding.

Bashō's mature haiku deal with basic matters. If he declares himself alone, that means resolutely alone in the vast emptiness of outer space, not just sad and bereft. Autumn is the season of *sabishisa,* which means "loneliness" in ordinary usage, but "alone and rooted in the essential self" for the poet and Zen student. It is the Buddha under the bodhi tree before he rose to seek out his five disciples. It is Gandhi meditating in his ashram before leading the Salt March. It is the Arhat in his lonely forest cell.

Wu-men's poem at the end of his introduction to his *Wu Men Kuan* reads:

> The great way has no gate;
> There are a thousand paths.
> Once you pass the barrier
> You walk the universe alone.[6]

"The great way has no gate"—it is completely open. It is the *mumonkan,* the gateless barrier. "There are a thousand paths"—more than that! There are 84,000 delusive paths according to classical Buddhism, which become 84,000 ways to realization. "Once you pass the barrier / You walk the universe alone." D. T. Suzuki translates the last line: ". . . in royal solitude you walk the universe."[7]

In "This Road," Bashō's reflection is the quiet time of the mature man or woman, the interval of zazen for the Zen student, or, more essentially, the fundamental condition of the human being—always alone.

A monk asked Pai-chang: "What is a matter of special wonder?"
Pai-chang said: "Sitting alone at Ta Hsiung Peak."[8]

Ta Hsiung Peak was the location of Pai-chang's monastery. Yasutani Hakuun Rōshi comments about this case: "He is sitting alone in the universe of his belly. He lies down alone at Ta Hsiung Peak. He walks alone at Ta Hsiung Peak. Wherever, no one goes with him. He goes out alone; he returns alone. He is entirely alone! . . . 'Above the heavens, below the heavens, only I, alone and sacred.' "[9]

You are born alone, you have realization alone, you die alone. It is said that when the Buddha was born, he took seven steps in each of the cardinal directions, pointed one finger aloft and another down, and declared: "Above the heavens, below the heavens, only I, alone and sacred."[10]

This condition may be that of the Arhat in his forest cell, but Pai-chang's response also becomes a teaching for that untrained monk and for the rest of us, and Bashō's experience becomes a haiku. This spirit of sharing is the spirit of the Bodhisattva, saving all beings. True aloneness is with, as well as in, the universe.

In his translation "No one goes along this way but I," Miyamori interpolates "but I" as do some other translators. Although Bashō does not specify himself in the original, he is not absent. Anything but. The poet and the student of religion have a strong sense of self as the agent of realization.

Please do not misunderstand. When teachers of religion speak of getting rid of the self, they are referring to an experience, the momentary (though perhaps repeated) "shedding of body and mind," to use Dōgen's expression.[11] What is the self that experiences this? Bashō resolves that question clearly. It is "This road!" What is the self that reflects upon it? It is the poet himself, of course, with brush, ink, and paper at hand. With true experience, there is confident reflection.

> Let's play King
> Of the Mountain—
> Can you push me off?

ELEVEN

The Morning Glory and the Butterfly

The morning glory!
This too cannot be
My friend.

Asagao ya	Morning glory!
kore mo mata waga	this too also my
tomo narazu	friend cannot be

THE FORM   The cutting word *ya* at the end of the first segment indicates an "Ah!" experience on seeing the morning glory, and the next two segments are a reflection on the content of that experience. The subject of the verb *narazu*, "cannot be," is *kore*, "this." *Kore mo mata* means literally, "This too again."

COMMENT   Walter de la Mare comments somewhere in his

85

later writings that he discovered he was a very bright fellow when he was thirty. Well, on looking at the back of the card in my file for this "Morning Glory" poem, I find in my hand-writing the words: "Friendship really is full communication. The flower cannot serve us tea." Maybe I thought that was bright at the time, but I don't think so now, thirteen or fourteen years later. My idea was true enough, I suppose, but there is something much deeper.

With the *ya* we understand Bashō's experience to be "There is just that morning glory in the whole universe." Over and over Bashō encountered vivid phenomena, *that*. Just plop! Just the rising sun! Just the muddy melon! Each phenomenon is altogether independent and alone. Pure friendlessness. On the other hand, there is pure friendliness:

> Wake up! wake up!
> Be my friend
> Sleeping butterfly.

Oki yo oki yo	Wake up wake up
waga tomo ni sen	my friend be
neru kochō	sleeping butterfly

The words I translate as "my friend" are the same in both of these haiku. They may also be rendered "my companion."

How is it that the butterfly can be Bashō's friend, and the morning glory cannot? I am sure it is not that the butterfly is animate and free, and the flower is attached to its stem. I think the difference lies in the basic elements of deepest experience, individuality and equality.

> The clouds and the moon are the same;
> Valleys and mountains are different . . .
> All are blessed; all are blessed,
> Ten thousand blessings, ten thousand blessings;
> Is this one? Is this two? [1]

The butterfly asleep, poised on a leaf or branch, presents its own sphere of existence, separate from that of Bashō. That is the world of individuality, where there are no companions, a blessed world. But Bashō is saying that there is another blessed world, where the two of us may dart about together, the world of equality.

Wu-men's questions in the last line of his poem cannot be answered intellectually. Is this one? Is this two? We may experience the blessed world of individuality at one time and the blessed world of equality at another, but are they actually separate aspects or the same thing?

Bashō does not, of course, answer such a question, or even pose it. However, throughout his later work he shows us individuality and equality, now one side, now the other, now both together (as in the "Sleeping Butterfly"). An example of the individual side would be "This Road," which we examined in the last chapter. At the end of his life, Bashō wrote: "Autumn deepens / My neighbor— / What does he do?" and this is a fine example for the side of equality. On his deathbed, he reached out for the sangha.[2]

The friendlessness of Bashō in the "Morning Glory" poem and his friendliness in "Sleeping Butterfly" are not simply opposite things of the relative world. The friendlessness of the morning glory and of Bashō are the fundamental aloneness in which each of us is born, in which each of us lives, and in which each of us dies. It is "sitting alone at Ta Hsiung Peak."

Each individual entity is its own reason for being, existing in its own impenetrable sphere. This is not the realm of selfishness, where I seek ascendancy over people about me. It is the realm of total solitude, where there are no people, animals, plants, or things anywhere in the vast, empty cosmos. This is the world where the morning glory cannot be Bashō's friend. There is only Bashō in the whole universe. There is only the morning glory in the whole universe.

The friendliness of Bashō and the potential friendliness of the butterfly present the other configuration of deepest experience. Each point in the infinitely broad and complex Net of Indra reflects each other point in "mutual and unhindered interpenetration of all existences."[3] We are all, as Nakagawa Sōen Rōshi once said, "members of the same nose-hole society." More intimate than sisters and brothers, as those words are ordinarily understood, each of us is kin by our fundamental sameness and equality to everyone and everything else.

With this realization, the world of the Bodhisattva appears. The recognition of one's own absolute and total uniqueness is also the compassionate acknowledgement of the absolute and total uniqueness of each other being, and of one's absolute equality with all of them.

Here are more examples of complete aloneness and of Indra's Net, expressed with Bashō's inimitable lightness and love:

> Morning glories
> Ignorant of carousing
> Are in full bloom.

Asagao wa	Morning glories:
sakamori shiranu	carousing don't know
Sakari kana	full bloom!

There is neat alliteration between *sakamori* and *sakari*— "carouse" and "bloom"—linking these two disparate activities as activities, however different.

People are hung over in their own sphere. The morning glories bloom vigorously in their own sphere. Not only morning glories, but children and other people, animals, and things that did not take part in the drinking are all in their individual worlds. The eight-year-old child who has any gumption at all will get up at the usual time, tiptoe through the drunken sleepers, make a solitary breakfast, and get out of the house as quickly as possible.

Baby mice in their nest
Squeak in response
To the young sparrows.[4]

Suzumego to	Young sparrows
koe nakikawase	voices cry in response
nezumi no su	mice of nest

Not only baby mice and baby sparrows, but all people, animals, and things are intimately interconnected. The word "symbiotic" means the living together in mutual dependence of dissimilar organisms. That says it all. We are all of us completely and absolutely dissimilar, living in complete and absolute dependence upon one another. We are a symbiotic universe, a symbiotic family of nations, a symbiotic country, state of that country, island, community, family, and even individual (for we have all kinds of creatures living in our insides).

Our Zen practice takes us deeply into this complementarity of aloneness and oneness. The very word "koan" is an illustration. *Kō* means "open to all," and the common usage of the ideograph is to mean "public." *An* means "case," as in "law case," and, by extension, "document." D. T. Suzuki justifies the meaning "public document" for koan "because it serves as such in testing the genuineness of enlightenment a student claims to have attained."[5]

Well, maybe so. True enough in practice, perhaps, but what is the heart of that which is tested? In their discussion of Dōgen Zenji's term *genjō kōan,* Norman Waddell and Masao Abe say about the word *kōan:* "According to the earliest commentary on the *Shōbōgenzō,* by Kyōgō, the *kō* of koan means sameness or ultimate equality that is beyond equality and inequality, and *an* refers to 'keeping one's sphere.' Koan thus indicates the individuality of things' differences and the difference of things' sameness."[6]

"Buddha nature pervades the whole universe." This is *kō,*

the sameness that is beyond equality and inequality. "Existing right here now" is *an*, the distinctly individual, keeping one's own sphere.[7]

Bashō, I am convinced, had long since realized these basic configurations in himself and in all things. His joyous samādhi practice was to present them through haiku and through the teaching of haiku, while living the solitary life of a pilgrim. It was a fulfilling life, and while yours and mine will be much different, such realization can bring fulfillment to us as well.

> It is not the ghost
> Of my father that walks
> On Waimanalo Beach.

TWELVE

The Four-and-a-Half-Mat Room

Autumn nearing
Inclination of my mind!
A four-and-a-half-mat room.

Aki chikaki	Autumn nears
kokoro no yoru ya	mind of inclination!
yojō han	four mats half

THE FORM   The first segment, "Autumn nearing," modifies the second, "inclination of my mind!" "My mind's inclination as autumn nears" would be a watered-down interpretation. The *ya* establishes this mood as the subject of the poem, and it also serves as a particle of expectation, like a colon, that introduces the object of the longing: a four-and-a-half-mat room.

COMMENT   Bashō was on his last journey when he composed this haiku. In failing health, he died only a few months later. It seems a presage of his last autumn, one of several haiku of this time that hint of an awareness of imminent death.

The four-and-a-half-mat room is the tea-ceremony room. One tatami mat is approximately three feet by six feet, so a room with four and a half mats is about nine feet square. Some tearooms are larger, and some even smaller, but Bashō's reference is to the classical size. A host and perhaps four guests might fit comfortably.

Though sometimes a tearoom forms part of an ordinary dwelling, more properly it is a separate hut consisting of just a single room. One reaches it through a garden decorated with stones, moss, and a brook. Often it is set near one or two pine trees. It is of fragile construction: usually mud and wattle walls, and a bark or grass roof. The entrance is very low, so that one must crawl in on hands and knees.

Inside, there is no decoration except for a tiny alcove with a simple flower arrangement and perhaps a single piece of calligraphy. A slender, unfinished post, chosen for its interesting form, sets off the alcove. The walls and ceiling are irregular in dimension and texture, mud plaster contrasting with woven wooden strips and untreated wooden panels. The windows have carefully crafted grilles made of reeds or twigs, and the light is very subdued.

There is usually a small hearth set in the floor, or a portable brazier set on the tatami. A venerable iron kettle is simmering as the guests enter, its sound echoing the wind in the pine trees outside. Greetings are limited to bows, and the guests sit silently as the host mixes the powdered tea and hot water in the time-honored ceremony. The guests are served the thick green tea broth and drink in turn—first one guest, then the next, and the next. After this, there is usually a little conversation, perhaps about the provenance of the tea bowl or the calligraphy in the alcove. It is quietly paced conversation, with silence between the words.

Myōan Eisai (1141–1245), founder of Japanese Rinzai Buddhism, is credited with introducing tea plants into Japan in the early thirteenth century, though tea itself was known before his time. He considered it medicine that enhanced zazen, and the first tea ceremony was the practice of monks drinking from a large bowl and passing it from hand to hand as they sat facing an image of Bodhidharma.[1] Gradually, the drinking of tea became secularized, but to this day, even in an ordinary Japanese home, it has not completely lost its original spirit of religious communion.

Sen no Rikyū (1521–91), who brought the tea ceremony to a point of cultural fulfillment, lived just a hundred years before Bashō, and the tea ceremony was still vigorous in Bashō's time. Although Rikyū said that the purpose of tea ceremony is simply boiling water, making tea, and drinking it,[2] hidden in his words is the deepest kind of human experience, the sharing of that experience, and the interpenetration of "I" with earth, water, fire, and wind. Indeed, in his book *Zen and the Fine Arts,* Shin'ichi Hisamatsu argues that tea ceremony is Zen adapted for the mass of Japanese lay people.[3]

When Bashō wrote his "Autumn Nearing" haiku, the season of summer had begun perceptibly to incline toward autumn, and Bashō's mind inclines toward the end, toward communion in death. He longs for the deep harmony of old friends and the shared pleasure in the sound of the wind, the sigh of the kettle, and the plain, lovely forms of bowls and implements moving through the simple ceremony.

Bashō did not seek complete isolation. The way of haiku, and of Zen, is the tao of the universe, which contains all things. Even when he was secluded, he found himself relating to objects around him:

> Winter seclusion—
> Once again let me adjust myself
> To this post.

Fuyugomori	Winter seclusion
matayori sowan	once again will adjust to
kono hashira	this post

All the English translations of this poem that I could trace use the verb "will lean," or an equivalent, for *sowan*. The original is the hortative, or wishful, form of a verb meaning "accompany, suit, meet, to be adjusted to." "Let me once again be companion to this post" might be a possible translation.

Even when winter enforces his seclusion, Bashō maintains friendly relationships. He is always alone, as you and I are, but in his serenity he is confirmed by all things.

Here is a third haiku by Bashō, illustrating his deep feeling for the sangha. He wrote it on his deathbed, a few days before the end:

> Autumn deepens
> My neighbor—
> What does he do?

Aki fukaki	Autumn deepens
tonari wa nani wo	neighbor: what
suru hito zo	do person?

In the loneliest circumstance the human spirit can experience, Bashō's mind goes out to his neighbor, and almost artlessly he sets forth a poem on this movement of his mind. Subjective as always, this haiku is a classic expression of the human mind at rest, coming forth with concern, as R. H. Blyth says, to inquire: "How is my neighbor passing through the world?"[4]

Simone Weil makes a similar point: "In the first legend of the Grail, it is said that the Grail . . . belongs to the first comer who asks the guardian of the vessel, a king three-quarters paralyzed by the most painful wound, 'What are you going through?' ''[5] It is in our concern for others that we find the Grail.

Bashō's death related somehow to his digestive tract and a good deal of pain was involved. But even pain and the isolation forced by his illness did not turn his energy to his small self. His energy was directed outside, and we sense that he wanted to direct our attention to this inclination of his mind.

Religion and poetry are associated with the inner life, but that should not mean self-preoccupation. In Zen we learn that inside and outside are not two, and Basho's inquiry about his neighbor reveals his acute awareness of this fact, undiminished and vital in spite of his circumstances. Though he was unable to express himself with his usual vigor, still his mind was not disrupted, and, if this poem is any indication, surely he maintained his intimate relation with all things into death itself.

It is this same intimacy of relationship that is manifested in the poems about the post and the four-and-a-half-mat room. The post is not an inanimate prop, a mere adjunct of human life, but rather a fondly remembered and respected being in its own right, a friend. And Bashō's inclination toward the simplicity, beauty, and social concord of tea ceremony is pure expression of the Bodhisattva's longing for his true home of perfect harmony.

Looking at the dialogues of Zen, we find them all to be expressions of Bodhisattvas enjoying this true harmony—or seeking it, anyway. One of my favorites is the encounter of Liu T'ieh-mo and Kuei-shan Ling-yu, two old friends, a nun and a priest, equal in realization, with nothing to prove and just the precious treasure of treasures to toss back and forth.

When T'ieh-mo appeared, Kuei-shan greeted her, saying: "T'ieh-mo! You old buffalo! So you have come!" (This was not condescending, for the water buffalo is a splendid creature, powerful and resolute, often considered in China and Japan to symbolize Buddha nature itself. You may suppose that Kuei-shan is simply giving his old friend an affectionate greeting. But more is involved. What is that hidden element?)

T'ieh-mo replied: "There is a great charity meeting tomorrow at Mount T'ai. Will Your Reverence be going?" (We are told that Mount T'ai was a vast distance from Kuei-shan's monastery. What is T'ien-mo's intention in asking such a silly question?)

Kuei-shan responded to it by throwing himself to the floor. (This seemingly absurd action was also part of the sequence that both of them understood.) When she saw this, T'ieh-mo walked out, and that was the end of the encounter.[6]

Some people say that koans are stale old exercises that obscure the living fact of realization. If one takes them in that spirit, they probably are. Some people say that tea ceremony is a contrived ritual of rich people pretending to be in harmony with nature and each other. That is one way to look at it, and not altogether untrue in some instances.

"How do you do?" "Thank you." These expressions can be cheap and meaningless, but only for people who have lost the touchstone of humanity. I show you my touchstone: "How do you do?" You show me yours: "Thank you very much."

When the weather is warm, we like to go to the beach together, and this experience is fellowship in fine weather. But when the weather is cool and rainy, we stay at home and have tea. This is another kind of fellowship. There are fewer distractions, and the sound of the rain and the quiet conversation we enjoy are a treasure that is deeply meaningful. How else may we find our pleasure here?

> I'm sorry to hear he died.
> Thank you very much—
> Let me serve you tea.

THIRTEEN

Bush Clover and the Moon

At the same inn
Play women too were sleeping;
Bush clover and the moon.

Hitotsu ya ni	One inn at
yūjo mo netari	play women too were sleeping
hagi to tsuki	bush clover and moon

THE FORM   The first two sections give the factual situation, which Bashō presents in a simple, straightforward way. The third is a kind of counterpoint or apposition: "Bush clover and the moon." The essence of the poem lies in the relationship between this last line and the preceding description.

COMMENT   Bashō wrote this poem at age forty-five or so, three years after "The Old Pond" and well into his poetical prime. It appears in his travel diary *The Narrow Way Within*, which provides background information that is helpful in considering this haiku.[1]

According to the story, the complete text of which is available in Donald Keene's *Anthology of Japanese Literature*,[2] it seems that Bashō and his companion Sora reached an inn one evening after a long day of travel. They went to bed soon after their arrival, but were kept awake for a while by conversations in a nearby room, which they could hear clearly through the paper partitions. Two women were discussing their impending separation the next day from their elder escort, and they were giving him letters and many verbal messages for friends at home.

It seems that these two women regarded themselves as victims of bad karma, as wrecks washed to a beach by white waves, and they feared retribution in the next world. They were on pilgrimage to the Grand Shrine of Ise, the center of worship for the Shinto religion.

The next morning the women asked the two poets' permission to follow them at a distance for the protection their black priest robes might afford. However, the two poets planned many detours from the main road and advised the women to find other, more reliable companions. The poets felt sad at the situation of these pathetic people.

Prostitutes in Japan are certainly beyond the pale socially, but there is not the feeling we find in the West that they are totally degraded and corrupt. The etymological difference between "prostitute" and "play woman" is revealing in this respect. Play women are often the subject of poetry and romantic fiction, and are usually treated with a modicum of dignity and humanity. Japanese people regard them much in the way our Victorian ancestors regarded circus performers or professional dancers on the popular stage.

Bashō was moved by the humanity of the women, and at the same time he felt the contrast implicit in the situation: two grizzled old poets sleeping at the same inn with exotics of the floating world of entertainment and easy love. His clear statement of the scene makes an interesting beginning for his poem, and scholars find little to differ about in those first two segments. It is with "Bush clover and the moon" that they diverge in explication.

There are three possible interpretations of that line. First, Bashō equates himself with the moon, serene and aloof, sailing through the sky, while putting the play women on a level with the unfortunate, humble bush clover, living out its brief karma down below.[3] The second, and much sounder interpretation, I think, is that the line simply denotes the mildly humorous juxtaposition of widely disparate things.[4] The third interpretation would be that of Zen.

When the great Fa-yen Wen-i pointed to bamboo blinds, two monks went and rolled them up simultaneously and in the same way. Fa-yen said: "One gains; one loses."[5] Like Bashō as the moon and play women as bush clover, this seems an obvious case of comparison. But if it were comparison, what would be so significant about it? Comparisons are odious— they have no metaphoric content, no inner life. They are entirely conceptual, for they place things and people in mental categories, by their very nature superficial and often destructive.

No, it is clear that Fa-yen was not being merely comparative. He was not judging one monk in relation to the other. Fundamentally, there is no loss and no gain, as ancient sutras and modern physicists keep telling us.

Jesus said: "Judge not, that ye be not judged."[6] This ordinarily is understood to mean: "Do not judge, or God will judge you." We can also understand it to mean "Don't judge because that puts you in the conceptual framework of right and wrong, gain and loss, saint and ordinary person, satori and ignorance, and so on." How much better if we can see, as the Japanese proverb says: "The crow goes caw-caw and the sparrow goes chirp-chirp."

It is much too conceptual to say that Bashō is the moon and

the women are bush clover. Any metaphor is true only at the level of experience. It dies in a philosophical setting. To show how the metaphor is the juxtaposition of two widely separate things would be a step in the right direction, but it still does not present the deepest possibility. We must see the elements as *that* before the haiku truly makes sense.

Question: What is the significance of play women and Bashō?
Answer: Bush clover and the moon!

Bashō has entangled a few scholars by giving them something to interpret, but his fundamental intention is right there on the surface. Fa-yen, likewise, was entirely straightforward: one gains, one loses.

> The moon shines fully
> Only once a month:
> Don't miss that chance!

FOURTEEN

The Goi

A flash of lightning;
Through the darkness goes
The scream of a night heron.

Inazuma ya   Lightning!
yami no kata yuku   darkness of side goes
goi no koe   night heron of cry

THE FORM   *Yami no kata* literally means "from the side of darkness"—in other words, from the side of the dark, not from the side of light. *Yuku* means "go" but, unlike its English equivalent, is never used to indicate the expression of an animal's sound, as in our idiom "the dog goes bowwow." The original simply implies passage of the sound through the darkness.

COMMENT This is another of Bashō's last haiku, written during a visit to his native village of Iga, a month or so before his death in Osaka. In the charged silence of the coming autumn storm, he lies comfortably suspended in the darkness. Suddenly the lightning flashes, and through the darkness that returns, the night heron screams its response.

In Christianity, darkness denotes sin and error, but for the poet and the student of religion in Asia, darkness is an organic metaphor of the undifferentiated absolute, while light is the experience of the immediate, phenomenal world. Absorbed in the darkness, Bashō is absorbed in the universe, timeless, without bounds. Suddenly, out of the blackest depths comes that extraordinary blaze of light, and the whole world of particulars is etched at once, chillingly, in his mind. Then darkness returns, and from that absolute vacancy again there is vivid eruption, this time an eerie scream.

Such is the nature of our deepest experience. Calling and answering may be seen superficially as cause and effect, but when I say "How are you?" there is only that question, emerging from the darkest unknown. When you reply "Pretty well," there is only that response, appearing from the void. Out of silence comes sound; out of darkness comes light. The silence charges the sound; the darkness charges the light.

Integration of the universal and the particular is essential to finding fulfillment in our lives. The great challenge to humanity is how to deal with particulars in view of the universal—in view of the fact of essential nature—and this is why Zen has so much to teach us. Formal Zen practice is taken up entirely with experiences of the universal and the particular, with the recognition of their interpenetration, and with the application of such experiences and insights in everyday life.

In the dedication of our sutras, the leader reads: "Buddha nature pervades the whole universe, / Existing right here now."[1] The first line is the universal, the absolute, the dark, the silent. The second line is the particular, the immediate, the phenomenal. Buddha nature, self nature, reality, whatever we choose to call it, is now dark, now vivid, now silent, now crackling with sound. It is light within the darkness, darkness within the light; it is just the darkness, just the light; it is darkness as the light.

Tung-shan Liang-chieh established five degrees of interfusion of the universal and the particular in Zen experience as the *Wu Wei* (Goi, or Five Degrees).* These are the particular within the universal, the universal within the particular, emerging from the universal, arriving from the particular, and the universal together with the particular.[2]

In such abstract terms, this classification seems dry and insubstantial, but the words are rooted through sight, hearing, taste, smell, touch, and awareness, to deepest experience. The light of the particular flashes from the dark of the universal. The darkness returns, and a night heron screams from the universe. In these immediately consecutive experiences, the scream and the lightning are one with the darkness, and the sighs of the poet and reader alike.

The relationship of words and experience is revealed particularly in this haiku by the name of the night heron, the *goi,* identical in Japanese in pronunciation and ideographs to the Goi of Tung-shan. In one respect, it is the Five Degrees of the universal and particular that crash through the darkness and silence in Bashō's experience, and Bashō has reflected this insight in his poem by allowing the double meaning of *goi.* Had he wanted simply the night heron to appear, he probably would have rendered the word in *kana,* the Japanese phonetic characters. Instead, he used Chinese ideographs, in which both meanings of the word are present, with Tung-shan's Five Degrees as a distinct shadow of the first meaning, "night heron." We can be certain that this choice was a conscious one for Bashō, because in writing other haiku, he played openly with

* Taizan Maezumi, Rōshi of the Zen Center of Los Angeles, translates *Goi* as "Five Positions" to avoid the connotation of progression.

these options—using Chinese characters for a certain expression in one version and Japanese phonetics for that same expression in another version, thereby clearly altering the sense of the poem.

Apparently, the Five Degrees of Tung-shan were not actually part of formal Zen practice in Bashō's time, but were incorporated into the practice by Hakuin, who was born in 1686, when Bashō was forty-two years old. However, we know that the Five Degrees were familiar to Japanese Zen teachers as early as the thirteenth century, and they were undoubtedly a part of the intellectual equipment of people such as Bashō, educated in Chinese classics and trained in Zen Buddhism.[3]

Bashō had probably long ago appreciated the possibility of a wordplay involving the two discrete meanings of *goi,* but only in the context of truly penetrating experience did he take up this wordplay, and then only to enrich his poem by adding the resonance of insight to an already vivid presentation of experience.

Bashō was not indulging in empty, intellectual association. Such nonsense is the bane of our lives, obscuring the clear fact of *that,* and indeed Bashō warns of such rootless associational thinking in another haiku:

> How noble—
> The one who is not enlightened
> At a flash of lightning!

Inazuma ni	Lightning at
satoranu hito no	does not satori person of
tōtosa yo	nobility!

This didactic poem has appeared in several English translations, three of them by R. H. Blyth, who renders it, with slight variations: "How admirable / He who thinks not, 'Life is fleeting,' / When he sees the lightning!"[4]

Though such a translation deviates considerably from the

original, it hints at Bashō's intention. The *Diamond Sutra* says that life is like dew, a shadow, or a flash of lightning, and Bashō is here commending those who do not fix on such words, deluding themselves with them, intellectually dredging up a realization of life's ephemerality at every lightning bolt. It is a noble person whose feet are firmly on the ground—who is not given to wandering in ethereal abstractions.

Bashō is not denying that a flash of lightning may enlighten you, but he is warning that one should be careful of convention, of the Five Degrees, and of the *Diamond Sutra*. Rootless talk of satori and the sound of a stone striking bamboo, the association of worldly affairs with drops of dew, and all the other endless conventions of illuminative expression are conceptual and shallow. Life is too short for metaphysics, as Inspector French would say.

Bashō's use of *goi*, on the other hand, is a stroke of genius. I am sure he knew Tung-shan inside out, and the Five Degrees were completely integrated in his own deepest consciousness. The scream of the night heron brought them incisively forth as a single realization for us to experience. If we can balance this interpretation with Bashō's own caution not to be used by association, then we have cause to venerate our ancestors.

> The white-eye comes to feed
> On a spray of elderberries;
> Hangs there, flies away.

FIFTEEN

Traveler

Let my name
Be traveler;
First rains.

Tabibito to　　　　　　"Traveler"
waga na yobaren　　　 my name let be called
hatsu shigure　　　　　first rains

THE FORM   The *to* at the end of the first segment is equivalent to quotation marks: let my name be "Traveler."

COMMENT   *Hatsu shigure* are the first rains of winter. Bashō was about to set out for his birthplace in Iga, near Kyoto, from his hermitage in Edo. He was forty-three and had written "The Old Pond" a year earlier. Certainly only one rightly named

106

"Traveler" would undertake such a long journey on foot at the beginning of winter.

In his *The Narrow Road Within,* Bashō speaks of poets and pilgrims who died on the road, and at the beginning of still another pilgrimage, in a haiku I cited earlier, he writes of his own determination to follow their example:

> I am resolved
> To bleach on the moors;
> My body is pierced by the wind.

Nozarashi wo	Moor-bleached—
kokoro ni kaze no	mind in wind of
shimu mi kana	pierce body!

This haiku breaks after *ni* (in), while *kaze no* (wind's) is the start of the second clause. Thus it is an interesting example of meaning in two parts laid over the haiku and its form, which is in three parts. The wording is elliptical and means: "My body is pierced by the wind and I am determined to bleach my bones on the moors." Absolute for death, Bashō is determined to carry his pilgrimage to the ultimate.

Such vivid expression of determination is peculiarly Japanese, but the tradition for arduous pilgrimage is rooted in Chinese Buddhism and in earlier Indian tradition. Many koans relate to pilgrimage. Huang-po Hsi-yun addressed his assembly and said: "You are all eaters of brewer's dregs. If you go about on pilgrimage as you do, when can you meet today?"[1]

There is more to this koan, but this is enough for our purposes. Brewer's dregs are edible, but they are fermented and smell to high heaven. During World War II, the Japanese made patties out of the dregs of imitation sakè—I think potatoes were the original ingredient. We internees called them "*benjo*-burgers"—*benjo* being the "place of convenience," which in our camp smelled about the same as the patties.

Anyway, Huang-po is saying that you cannot meet today,

you cannot meet this moment, if you just wander around consuming smelly secondhand truths. When Nanch'uan P'u-yuan was a young monk, it was thought that one's training was incomplete without an interview with then the imperial tutor, Nan-yang Hui-chung. This poor old teacher got pasted into a lot of scrapbooks, I'm afraid.[2]

Yun-men's intention was similar to that of Huang-po when he scolded Tung-shan Shou-ch'u: "Oh you rice bag! Have you been wandering about like that, now west of the river, now south of the lake?"[3]

Huang-po and Yun-men take their students to task for their style of wandering, their spirit, their attitude—not for the wandering itself. What is our life but coming and going, after all? Bashō was compelled to wander all over Japan; Thoreau was compelled to wander in Concord.

At the farewell party the night before Bashō set out for Iga, the group composed a renku. Bashō's "Traveler" verse was the hokku, the first line of seventeen syllables:

> Let my name
> Be traveler;
> First rains.

His host then capped this verse with a second line of fourteen syllables:

> May you have camellia flowers
> As shelter, night after night.

| *Mata tsubaki ka wo* | Again camellia flowers |
| *yado yado ni shite* | shelter shelter as make |

The long poem continued, with other members of the party adding lines of seventeen, then fourteen syllables, until the renku was completed. Seasonal references to early winter in "early rains" and "camellia flowers" formed one link between Bashō's verse and that of his host. Other links, of course, are references to the forthcoming journey, and to Bashō himself.

We may appreciate the host's genteel concern that Bashō have aesthetic shelter each night, but deeper still we can discern the essential pattern of life itself. On the one hand, Bashō wandered, as all of us wander. But if camellias do not punctuate our wandering, we are only potato bags, and our pilgrimage will not truly reveal the mind of the imperial tutor.

Bashō set out for scenic and historical places, but he usually did not write about them. He wanted to see them, all right, but they became simply turn-around places. Like retirement ceremonies, they had no great significance, and it was points on the journey that provided him with so much inspiration:

> Coming along the mountain path
> I find something endearing
> About violets.

Yamaji kite	Mountain path coming
naniyara yukashi	somehow endearing
sumire gusa	violets

I first read this haiku in Miyamori's anthology almost forty years ago, and I have not yet used up its evocative spirit. Now I can see more deeply, however: "Going and coming, never astray."

That is the heart of it. As Bashō wandered, it was just the violets. Just the sun popping up. Just (on one occasion) his falling from his horse. As Yamada Kōun Rōshi says: "Just standing up. Just sitting down. Just laughing. Just weeping." It is only that endearing emotion, nothing else! Just those violets, nothing else!

I meet lots of rice bags—scrapbook students of religion. "I studied with so-and-so rōshi at such-and-such center, and he has this-and-that style of teaching. Then I went to see so-and-so *rimpoche*"—and on and on it goes. There is a subtle but essential difference between such wandering and true pilgrimage. Even the great Chao-chou Ts'ung-shen, who wandered twenty years, was challenged on this point:

When Chao-chou called upon Yun-chu Tao-ying, the latter asked: "Oh, you old wanderer, why don't you find yourself a home?"

Chao-chou said: "Where is my home?"

Yun-chu said: "There is a ruined temple at the foot of this mountain."

Chao-chou said: "That is a good place for Your Reverence."

Later he came to Tsung Yung-shan, who asked: "Oh, you old wanderer, why don't you settle down?"

Chao-chou said: "Where should I settle down?"

Tsung Yung-shan said: "Why, this old wanderer doesn't even know where to settle down!"

Chao-chou said: "I have been training horses for thirty years, and today I get kicked by a donkey."[4]

Bashō's host was better than Yun-chu here. Yun-chu was an excellent master, but even Homer nods, and he forgot momentarily that our home is in the experience of camellias or violets. Chao-chou appreciated the swift kick he got from Tsung Yung-shan, who knew a good target when he saw one.

But the Chinese master who can shake hands most firmly with Bashō is Ch'ang-sha Ching-ts'en, originator of the koan about stepping from the top of a hundred-foot pole:

One day Ch'ang-sha went on a jaunt to the mountains. When he returned to the gate, the head monk asked him: "Your Reverence, where have you been wandering?"

Ch'ang-sha said: "I have been strolling about in the hills."

The head monk said: "Where did you go?"

Ch'ang-sha said: "First I went following the scented grasses; then I returned following the falling flowers."

The head monk said: "That is very much a spring mood."

Ch'ang-sha said: "It is better than the autumn dew falling on the lotus blossoms."[5]

Several points are raised for koan study in this dialogue, but for our purposes the significant portion is Ch'ang-sha's response: "First I went following the scented grasses; then I returned following the falling flowers." Yamada Kōun Rōshi told me that sometimes this lovely line is quoted in the eulogy at a monk's funeral. It is the life of the mature Zen student, never astray amidst all the coming and going. It is the life of Bashō, singling out moments of eternity while wandering.

> The spring mood
> Comes and goes
> In November rains.

SIXTEEN

Hailstones

Look, children,
Hailstones!
Let's rush out![1]

Iza kodomo	Look children
hashiri arukan	let's rush out
tama arare	jewel hail

THE FORM   *Iza* is an exclamation that is not really translatable. It is variously rendered "Come! Look! Now then! Well now!" *Hashiri aruku* is a compound verb that means literally, "rush and go." The *an* ending puts it into the imperative, "Let's rush out!"

COMMENT   I have used R. H. Blyth's translation of this haiku. It seems to imply that Bashō is indoors with young friends. Perhaps the storm ends, and they run outside with him to see the hail piled up or to gather the hailstones.

Bashō's haiku are often sangha poems. In "Bush Clover and the Moon," prostitutes and poets are presented at a single inn. In "Autumn deepens . . . ," Bashō reaches out for his neighbor. In "Hailstones," Bashō partakes of the essential nature of children. The relationship is big child to little children, with nothing patronizing about it.

Human relations are more often the subject of senryū, the satirical verse form that usually follows the same syllabic count as haiku. Senryū are humorous, ironic, and sometimes patronizing, and they touch every facet of human life—marital relations, parent-child relations, in-law relations, neighbor relations, politics, trades, and so on. Here is a senryū that enters into the world of the child:

> My new mama
> Came from the Yoshiwara
> He says.[2]

Ima no kaka	"Present of mama-
san wa Yoshiwara	san: Yoshiwara
kara to ii	from" says

The Yoshiwara was the "gay quarters" in Edo. The child does not know this and would not understand its significance if he did. He is simply making a statement. He has a new mama and is excited about this great change in his life. But what can he say to express that excitement?

Somehow he picked up the word "Yoshiwara" with reference to her. It was weighted with importance when he heard it, and he feels that importance in his own way, as something he can say about her. Innocently, he is saying *something*. Zen literature is filled with similar innocent presentations of the fact itself.

But the adult acquaintance may not be so innocent, and one

can picture his sardonic expression as he smiles at the child and says: "Oh, that's nice!" The reader, too, smiles sadly. In senryū collections, this poem is placed in the section on mothers, not in the section on children. This epitomizes the attitude of senryū, which stands off like a camera and records with irony our human condition. The touch is light and a little cruel, and leaves us nodding regretfully.

Irony never participates. Apart and mocking, it cannot unite with its object. I wonder if I can go a step further and suggest that it is not possible to be separate in spirit without being judgmental.

Anyway, if a child said such a thing to Bashō, I am sure he would not make a poem about it. His haiku, and the tradition he established, do not concern themselves specifically with feelings of pity, smugness, envy, or whatever—nor with feelings of anger or love either. In this respect they are like Zen, as the *Cheng Tao Ke* (Song of Realization) tells us: "The Buddha's doctrine of directness / Is not a matter of human emotion."[3]

It is not a matter of ecstasy, not a matter open to argument. It is the fact. Just this, this! As an explanation, let us examine two aspects of Zen. On the one hand, there is the phenomenal world: it is born; it dies; it has color, quality, and form. On the other hand, there is the essential world: it is not born; it does not die; it has no quality, color, or form. The living unity of these two aspects is catching a bus or writing a letter home. Emphasis on human emotion puts stress upon the phenomenal side. It obscures the essential side, and makes difficult or impossible the oneness of emotion and realization that is found in life of the mature poet or Zen student.

There are many kinds of emotion. The aloof, sardonic spirit that patronizes the weakness of humanity is one; anger is another. Emotion is condition; it comes and goes, and usually has no lasting importance or significance. Taking it seriously for ourselves, or projecting it upon others, obscures the fact with which we must work. If someone comes to me and says, "I am very upset with you," then it is difficult to get at the point of disagreement. For many people, it is the anger that is important to express, not the point of contention. This attitude makes true sangha development very difficult.

Bashō, urging the children to rush out to enjoy the jewels of hail, himself became a child. He is neither recording the scene with mockery nor smothering us with emotion. He is a man playing with children, encouraging their enthusiasms, and presenting the experience for our participation as well.

Is that not emotion? No, I do not think so, not in the sense the *Song of Realization* meant, anyway. I think the passage refers to the emphasis on self-conscious feeling that some people seek in religion. It could also refer, of course, to the self-conscious, ironic spirit of the observer, to self-righteous anger of someone who is offended, and to self-indulgent love. Setting aside the aloof, critical human attitude for the moment, let us examine its opposite, the overwhelming projection. Recently one of my students asked me, quite out of the blue: "Do you love me?" I barely restrained myself from answering rudely in the negative.

We butter situations unrecognizably with love. Whereas on the one hand the adult reads associational meaning into the presentation of the child about his new mama, and so much the worse for that adult, what would the response of love be? I cannot say, but it seems to me that the true teacher would encourage the child to say more—"Does she tell you stories? Does she take you to the park?"—thus entering into the world of the child and encouraging him or her to be expressive, just as Bashō did.

Kanzeon neither stands aside nor broods about love. In Zen study, there are koans that relate to compassion, but never in expression, except in very roundabout ways, as when Ta-yu tells Lin-chi that the ninety blows he received from Huang-po were given in a most soft-hearted and grandmotherly way.[4]

What is it that kept Chao-chou going for his long life of

one hundred and twenty years? I deny that it was love. I deny that Kanzeon is self-conscious sangha spirit.

Kanzeon has a thousand arms and twenty-two eyes, and uses all those appurtenances wholeheartedly in the world. Rushing out to enjoy the hail with the children—this is one act of Kanzeon; coming to the zendō on Saturday morning to join with the sangha in painting and fixing—this is another act of Kanzeon. But these are not thoughtful actions. They are like reaching behind one's head for the pillow in the middle of the night, as an old teacher once said.[5]

Preoccupation with human foibles, as in senryū, binds all the hands and eyes of Kanzeon. The sophisticated neighbor, listening to the child tell of his new mama, has his mind everywhere except with that child.

On the other hand, the missionary of love has his or her eye simply on creating a certain emotion, smearing that emotion over the vital configurations of need that are everywhere. Thoreau says somewhere that he goes in the other direction when he sees someone coming to do him good. I told the student who tried to lay his big love trip on me: "There is no first principle, not love, not wisdom, not realization."

Bashō naturally chose the Middle Way. When the hail fell, he happened to be with a group of children. What did the great poet say?

> Look children!
> Hailstones!
> Let's rush out!

The error of the senryū approach is that it is aloof. The error of the big love trip is that it cannot relate to the needs of others. What is the Middle Way?

> Not wisdom, not love,
> Not seeing into essential nature,
> Certainly not eternal bliss.

Violets with calligraphy, by Bashō. . . . "Coming along the mountain path / I find something endearing / About violets." *(See page 109)*

Chuang-tzu and the Butterfly, by Ikeno Taiga. . . . The calligraphy reads: "If there were a voice / The man might be awakened / Flying butterfly." *(See page 125)*

SEVENTEEN

The Cricket

The cricket chirps
In a forgetful way:
This *kotatsu*![1]

Kirigirisu	Cricket
wasure ne ni naku	forget sound with cries
kotatsu kana	*kotatsu!*

THE FORM This verse builds toward the word *kotatsu*, as the final cutting word indicates, with each element modifying the next to create the final impact.

COMMENT The *kotatsu* is a uniquely Japanese architectural feature. It is an opening in the floor, usually three feet on each side and eighteen or so inches deep, located in a central place in the main room. A heater is placed in the hole—an electric coil nowadays, but a charcoal brazier in Bashō's time. A low table is placed over the hole, and a blanket or *futon* (quilt) covers the table, trailing generously over the tatami mat on all sides. Family members sit at the table with their feet in the hole and the futon drawn about their hips. Eight people can jam into this small space, and even more can share the warmth by kneeling outside the circle with an edge of the futon drawn over their knees. It is cold away from that kotatsu, so the natural tendency is to crowd in. It is not only the dining-room table: children do their homework there; adults use it for their drinking and gossiping; even the servant is part of it, not to mention the family cat, who often curls up in the hole. It is an important family center, but it is also a rather sleepy place.

Contentment, dreaminess, sleepiness—these are the inevitable associations of the kotatsu in Japanese poetry. In Bashō's haiku on the subject he is probably alone, and his mood of dreamy contentment is deepened by the chirp of a cricket, like the cricket on the hearth in Western literature. Mindlessly it chirps at irregular intervals. Certainly a full and complete presentation of the whole matter. Bashō finds his own forgetfulness in that chirp.

What relationship has this to Zen? One's mind turns to Zen art, where a number of paintings show masters sound asleep. One particular example by Shih-k'e is a Hotei-like figure asleep on a tiger, which is also asleep. In his caption to this painting, D. T. Suzuki says it is a "Zen father" in meditation.[2] But what kind of meditation? *ZZZzzz.*

As Keizan Jōkin says, most people want to have it pure white.[3] That is, most people have the idea that purity of condition is essential for true zazen. When we are on our cushions in the dōjō, we are told over and over that a dreamy condition is just as much a distraction as scheming, planning, random thoughts, or whatever. Perhaps it is. But dreaminess is at the same time a kind of zazen. Does this seem to be a paradox? It is a paradox of course, but paradox is something that appears with analysis. There is no paradox in nature.

The fact is that realization may be prompted by a dreamy condition, or by a thought, or by *makyō* (mysterious vision). Kenshō, the experience of seeing one's own nature, is most likely to occur after an intensive retreat is over. Without sincere, rigorous zazen, without earnest striving for that strip of white cloth, no experience is possible. This includes regular daily sitting, one-moment zazen at intervals of leisure during the day, and general avoidance of reckless activity that sets distracting karma in motion. But also, without the other side, without the flow of thoughts and feelings, no experience is possible. Our lives as Zen students are an ebb and flow.

Bashō's discipline was the pilgrimage and the exacting practice of writing haiku. But periodically he had to hole up. Periodically he had to take it easy and enjoy himself. Here is a summer poem with much the same spirit:

> How cool—
> A noonday nap
> With feet against the wall!

Hiya hiya to	Cool cool
kabe wo fumaete	wall against place feet
hirune kana	noon nap!

Japanese homes are traditionally wattle and mud, plastered inside and out. Like adobe, this is excellent construction for keeping people cool in summer, and the walls themselves are the coolest parts of the house. We may imagine the poet flat on his back, knees raised and his feet against the wall, snoozing through the heat of the day. A very endearing picture.

Western writers about Zen have sought to show how head monks in Japanese monasteries are stern with students who doze off during zazen. This may be true at some centers, but my experience is that leaders will simply tap the sleepy ones and admonish them quietly with one word such as "Steady!" Sometimes, at the beginning of a retreat when people have not yet caught their second wind, a head monk will patrol right past a line of students who are nodding with sleep, with never a word or a gesture.

According to Chinese records, Lin-chi I-hsuan once was dozing in the zendō. His teacher Huang-po came in to check on the monks. Seeing Lin-chi nodding there at his seat, Huang-po struck the edge of the sitting-platform with his staff. Crack! Lin-chi raised his head and saw it was Huang-po, then nodded off to sleep again.

Huang-po again struck the edge of the platform, and went on to the head monk. "That youngster in the lower part of the hall is meditating, what are you doing here with your head full of fantasy?" The head monk grumbled something, and Huang-po struck the edge once again and went out.[4]

The head monk in his zazen was not in as deep a condition as Lin-chi. Huang-po struck the edge of the platform, *crack,* to waken the head monk. You must become more sleepy!

Some people have a tendency to doze off every period of zazen. No sooner does the third bell of a period ring, than they are nodding. When they come to me with this supposed problem, I always assure them that the distraction of sleepiness is milder than the tendency during zazen to think about rearranging the furniture or to fantasize about telling off one's friend. The roof-brain is quiet, dream images come and go, and one is in a very settled condition. Hold your practice in that condition and you cannot go wrong. When you nod, come back to mu.

Drowsy contentment may be a condition close to realization. It is a kind of emptiness, of nondifferentiation, where the ten directions melt: inside and outside become one. A good *katsu* or the chirp of a gecko can do wonders then.

And that dreamy, contented condition is, of course, a model of enlightenment itself. It is "body and mind fallen away; the fallen away body and mind."* It is that very strip of white cloth itself. There is nothing at all in the whole universe, and one is sitting there, totally alone. Some students go through this dreamy, undifferentiated state as part of their ripening process. Here is an early haiku by Bashō that presents such a ripening condition beautifully:

A cloud of flowers —
Was that the bell of Ueno
Or Asakusa?

Hana no kumo	Flowers of cloud
kane wa Ueno ka	bell: Ueno?
Asakusa ka	Asakusa?

The poet is musing beneath a cloud of cherry flowers and the distant *bong* of a temple bell penetrates his consciousness. Deep in the undifferentiated aesthetic continuum, he is in the condition of a divine fool. "There was a temple bell. What direction did it come from? I don't know." Exactly the condition of the Zen master sleeping on a tiger.

Literal attitudes toward clarity, purity, silence, harmony, nonattachment, and so on can destroy the virtue of those qualities. It is true that we must be clear, but it may be the wandering thought that is a creative idea. Wu-men warns: "To be alert and never ambiguous is to wear chains and an iron yoke."[6] The *Ts'ai Ken T'an* (Vegetable Roots Discourses) tells us: "Water which is too pure has no fish."[7] Please be careful. The human way, the Buddha-tao, is the Middle Way. This is not the way of compromise with human frailty, but the way of realization and emancipation.

---

* The expression associated with Dōgen's realization experience.

Here is another of Bashō's haiku on this theme as a verse to end this chapter:

Summer in the world;
Floating on the waves
Of the lake.

Yo no natsu ya	World of summer!
kosui ni ukabu	lakewater on floating
nami no ue	waves of surface

In Japan, a popular translation of samsara *(waves of cause and effect) is ukiyo (the floating world). Bashō is literally floating in a boat, and he brings all the elements of ukiyo to his haiku—the world, floating, and the waves—in a beautiful expression of pleasure in our transient human life, which is none other than the Buddha.*

EIGHTEEN

Dreams

You are the butterfly
And I the dreaming heart
Of Chuang-tzu.

Kimi ya chō	You butterfly
ware ya Sōshi ga	I Chuang-tzu of
yume gokoro	dream mind

THE FORM   The two *ya* in this verse mean "and." This usage is common in literary Japanese when enumerating things of equal value. R. H. Blyth writes: "The two *ya*'s express the interpenetration of Sōshi and the butterfly, I and you."[1]

COMMENT   The reference here is, of course, to the passage in Chuang-tzu's writings that was as well known to Bashō and his friends as it is to us today: "Once Chuang Chou dreamt he was a butterfly flitting and fluttering around, happy with himself and doing as he pleased. He didn't know he was Chuang Chou. Suddenly he woke up and there he was, solid and unmistakably Chuang Chou. But he didn't know if he was Chuang Chou who had dreamt he was a butterfly or a butterfly dreaming he was Chuang Chou. Between Chuang-chou and a butterfly there must be *some* distinction! This is called the Transformation of Things."[2]

Chuang-tzu was an important Taoist teacher and writer who lived in the fourth century B.C., perhaps two hundred years after the semilegendary Lao-tzu. Clearly he was an influence upon the development of Zen Buddhism, a thousand and more years later. For example, the following passage from Chuang-tzu could be the words of any one of many Zen founders: "There is nothing in the world bigger than the tip of an autumn hair, and Mount T'ai is tiny. No one has lived longer than a dead child, and P'eng-tsu [the Chinese Methuselah] died young. Heaven and earth were born at the same time I was, and the ten thousand things are one with me."[3] This is a direct expression of the experience of Zen students today. But immediately following we find words that are uniquely Chuang-tzu—nobody else could say it like this: "We have already become one, so how can I say anything? But I have just *said* that we are one, so how can I be not saying something? The one and what I said about it make it two, and the two and the original one make three. If we go on this way, then even the cleverest mathematician can't tell where he'll end, much less ordinary people. If by moving from non-being to being we get to three, how far will we get if we move from being to being? Better not to move, but to let things be!"[4] In his own unique way, Chuang-tzu makes a pre-Zen statement of suchness, but he would never use such a word. Modern teachers will sometimes use technical words by way of explanation, but religious vitality is thereby lost to some degree.

A decline in religious expression can be discerned from Chuang-tzu, through the Ch'an Buddhism of the T'ang period

(618–906), through Zen of the Kamakura period (1185–1336), through Keizan (1267–1325), Hakuin (1685–1768), and finally to the koan answer book recently published by Basic Books.[5] Ta-hui Tsung-kao burned the printing blocks of the *Pi Yen Lu* (The Blue Cliff Record), a great Sung-period (960–1279) textbook of Zen compiled by his own beloved teacher. I do not know specifically what he said as he burned them, but my guess is that he believed he was destroying an enemy of Zen life.

But Zen lives. Bashō lives. His haiku about the heart-mind of Chuang-tzu was an occasional verse, sent to a friend named Doi who had given him a writing brush. As he often did, Bashō took inspiration from old writings and turned the entire idea completely about to make a new and fresh poem. While Chuang-tzu was playing with interpenetration and transformation of all things, but specifically himself and a butterfly, Bashō was playing with his friend, personalizing the sangha.

Bashō, the adult child who had long since entered the kingdom of heaven, said: "You're the butterfly, and I the dreaming heart of Chuang-tzu. I don't know if I'm Bashō who dreamed with the heart-mind of Chuang-tzu that I was a butterfly named Doi, or that winged Mr. Doi dreaming he is Bashō." How intimate. How happy his friend must have been.

As Chuang-tzu himself says: "Someday there will be a great awakening when we know that this is all a great dream. Yet the stupid believe they are awake, busily and brightly assuming they understand things, calling this man ruler, that one herdsman—how dense!"[6] This passage forms part of an attack on Confucius, who separated people by classes. The master goes on to say: "Confucius and you are both dreaming! And when I say you are dreaming, I am dreaming too! Words like these will be labeled the Supreme Swindle."[7]

But like Chuang-tzu and Bashō, we must use words. How should we use them? By playing with them, as they both did, and as did Huang-po, Yun-men, Ch'ang-sha, and countless other Zen teachers. The purpose is to present something, not to mean something. Meaning something destroys it. If Chuang-tzu had said "The butterfly and I are one," he would have expired on the spot, and nobody would have remembered him for longer than a week. If Bashō had said "I am you and you are I," his friend Doi would have demanded his brush back.

In sangha play, I make my presentation. I am Doi, giving you a brush. You make your presentation. You are Bashō, sending me a poem. In the dokusan room, you show me your treasure, then I show you my treasure. As Wu-men says, with no means for sustenance, we dare to compete with the other for riches:[8] A similarly playful sangha expression is found in Bashō's haiku:

> You kindle the fire;
> I'll show you something nice:
> A great ball of snow.

Kimi hi take	You fire light
yoki mono misen	nice thing will show
yukimaroge	snow ball

Yukimaroge is not an ordinary snowball, which is *yukidama* in Japanese; it is, rather, a great ball of snow, made by rolling and pushing. Japanese people are very fond of making such giant snowballs, and there are several haiku on the subject in Japanese literature.

This poem is another expression of Basho's delight in intimate companionship and in intimate presentation. "While you are kindling the fire, I'll do my part and roll a big snowball. You present the fire; I present the snowball."

Many years ago at Koko An, Nakagawa Sōen Rōshi asked me: "What do you think is most important in the whole world?" As usual, I could not answer, and he said: "I suppose friends are most important in the whole world." We were old friends, and I was deeply moved. It is in friendship that the universe reflects itself.

Back in 1951, when I prepared to leave the Ryūtaku-ji monastery, Sōen Rōshi gave me a pottery tea bowl, one of a set of three of differing forms but similar glaze and pattern, made by the Tokyo potter Guro. The Rōshi had already given one of the bowls to G. Ray Jordan during his first visit to the United States in 1949. Whenever two of us meet, we bring our bowls and have ceremonial tea with them, as an expression of our brotherhood: the three bowls are known as the Brother Bowls. Only once in the over twenty-five years since the bowls were dispersed have all three brothers met together for such a ceremony, at the Ojai sesshin in 1968. At that time, the three of us exchanged bowls, so now I have a renewed symbol of our little sangha.

Tea ceremony is a solemn affair. No one speaks while the powdered tea is dipped out of the container, placed in the bowl, and mixed with the hot water. But it is play, nonetheless. All our sangha work is serious investment in the Dharma, but it is play. Bowing to the Buddha, I throw everything away. Offering incense and flowers, I take great care. Sitting on my cushions, I discipline myself just to sit, or to count my breaths, or to take up mu.

It is important that we take our practice and our sangha relations in this dynamic spirit. When things become grim in a discussion of zendō business, then it is time to go into meeting, as the Quakers say. They do this by sitting silently together in a spirit of devotion. Sometimes they hold hands. Thus the universe becomes transparent and all points reflect all other points. In that dream, sangha relations become complete.

There are different kinds of dreams. Sometimes there is a dream within a dream, as Wu-men tells us.[9] An old teacher asked: "What if someone came to you in a dream and said 'What is the meaning of Bodhidharma's coming from the West?' How would you respond? If you cannot answer, then Buddhism has no subtle power."[10] What is your presentation? You must sort out your dreams.

> All action is like a dream,
> A fantasy, a bubble, a shadow,
> A dewdrop, or a flash of lightning.[11]

NINETEEN

Cherry Blossoms

How many, many things
They bring to mind—
Cherry blossoms!

Samazama no	Many many of
koto omoidasu	things present to mind
sakura kana	cherry!

THE FORM *Samazama* is an expression meaning "many different kinds." This haiku is another that builds toward the final noun—in this case, *sakura*. The cutting word *kana* heightens the impact of the ending.

COMMENT Cherry-blossom time is a special event for Japanese people. If they possibly can, they make up picnic lunches on one of the few days the flowers are in their prime, and promenade and picnic under the trees. In cities, literally hundreds of thousands of people will visit a particularly famous grove at a park, shrine, or temple. Littlest children and oldest grandparents accompany their families on this modest pilgrimage each year. Time passes, and family associations with these excursions accumulate. As at Christmas or Thanksgiving in the West, it is an opportunity to enjoy for the present, and a time to recall other happy days too, when faces and laughter were seen and heard that will never be seen or heard again. Instilled in the Japanese mind is the association of the ephemerality of the cherry blossoms with the brevity of human life. Blooming for so short a time, and then casting loose in a shower of lovely petals in the early April wind, cherry blossoms symbolize an attitude of nonattachment much admired in Japanese culture.

In this verse, Bashō was on pilgrimage again, the same journey that he began with the poem "Let my name / Be traveler." Here he has arrived at his birthplace in Iga and is visiting the castle of Ueno, where he had served as a young man. Twenty years before, he had renounced the world when the young lord died and he lost his intimate companion and fellow poet. After a very long time he was home again, now as a poetry master. The cherry trees he loved as a boy and youth are in full bloom, and as he walks beneath them, he recalls many things he cannot bear to put into words.

Bashō himself is always the subject of his haiku, sometimes more personally and idiosyncratically than here. He never seemed to stray into indulgent self-consciousness in his mature poetry, but rather noted himself as an element he knew well in an environment of natural change. It is recollection that is central to this verse, recollection evoked by cherry blossoms.

When he walked beneath the trees in the castle garden, he was living once again those youthful days with his long-dead companion. Like all of us, he was not bound by time. The most vivid and most mysterious of such experiences we call déjà vu,

131

a kind of religious experience in which time and space are transcended. What I am and what I do are the same now as in the past, perhaps the dim, distant past. The past is the present; Newark is Paia; my old friend is my new friend.

One gets the impression that in Zen it is bad to maunder about in memories. It is just *this*, and so on—just this present moment, just this breath, just this koan. All right. How about just this memory? Would that not be all right too? Cherry-blossom time is a time for memories; family reunions are a time for memories. Zazen is a time for koan work. Breakfast is a time for porridge and fruit.

A monk asked Feng-hsueh Yen-chao: "Speech is a matter of subject and object. Silence is a matter of subject and object. How may I transcend subject and object?"

Feng-hsueh said: "I always think of Chiang-nan in March. Partridges chirp among the many fragrant blossoms."[1]

Sitting in his monastery, confronting students in Dharma battle, Feng-hsueh is in effect asked "What is not relative?" He replies by quoting lines of the poet Tu Fu, recalling another place and time. Was this not a relative answer?

The remarkable thing about déjà vu, or about other vivid experiences of recollection, is that they are vested with significance that we cannot put into words. At an earlier time, whatever happened might have seemed important, or it might not. But the recollection is charged with relevance, and tears flow for no reason. What is so relevant?

It touches the deepest place of all. Wu-men says there is "a spring that does not belong to yin and yang."[2] "Spring" here refers to season. Yin and yang form the basis of the *I Ching* (Book of Changes). Light and dark, positive and negative, giving and receiving, male and female—Wu-men says there is a spring that does not belong to such differentiation, or to changes or seasons. How do you show such a season?

I remember reading a poem by James Norman Hall many

years ago in which he described himself standing in the snow under a palm tree in Tahiti.[3] He had been a member of the Lafayette Escadrille in World War I, and, completely fed up with violence and Western culture, he had exiled himself to the South Seas when the war was over. But there in Tahiti, under a palm tree, he was knee-deep in snow. He had never left home at all.

Robert Louis Stevenson, an earlier exile in the South Seas, wrote at Vailima in Samoa about the hills of his home in Scotland:

> Blows the wind today, and the sun and the rain
>   are flying,
>   Blows the wind on the moors today and now,
> Where about the graves of the martyrs the whaups
>   are crying,
>   My heart remembers how!
>
> Grey recumbent tombs of the dead in desert places,
>   Standing stones on the vacant wine-red moor,
> Hills of sheep, and the homes of the silent
>   vanished races,
>   And winds, austere and pure:
>
> Be it granted to behold you again in dying,
>   Hills of home! and to hear again the call;
> Hear about the graves of the martyrs the
>   peewees crying,
>   And hear no more at all.[4]

The moors of Scotland in the rain forests of Samoa; the snow of North America among the palm trees of Tahiti; Chiang-nan in March in the midst of Dharma combat—here is Bashō again, this time finding lonely autumn evenings in the holiday season of the new year:

New Year's Day!
When I reflect—
Lonely autumn evenings.

Ganjitsu ya	New Year's Day!
omoeba sabishi	when I reflect, lonely
aki no kure	autumn of evening

This poem is difficult to render into English, so the meaning may not come through so sharply. The dash after "when I reflect" is the clue to the true significance of the poem. It is not that I remember loneliness, but it is rather that upon the act of reflection, I find lonely autumn evenings right here.

New Year's Day is another very happy time in Japan. Actually, the holiday extends over a period of days. Business stops completely; children and young women dress in their best clothing; people visit one another; rice wine flows freely. Nowadays, the great cold of mid-January is still to come, but under the old lunar calendar, New Year's Day was the beginning of spring. The plum blossoms were out, and the worst of winter was past. But old times or modern, it was and is an occasion of great celebration, of happiness in the present and anticipation of the future.

Bashō finds lonely autumn evenings in his mind at this time. He was in touch with the spring that transcends yin and yang. This group of friends, gathered here for a wedding, a dance, a holiday, will never again be a group together. All things in this floating world change and pass away. There will be new faces next time, and old ones will be gone. And it is not merely that the world is transitory. With that gaiety there is expression of the true season. When we ignore that season, our laughter is thin indeed. But acknowledging it, we can embrace it with tears of joy.

Manoa hills are misty with rain
And I recall a prisoner
Who longed to see them once more.

Goblin Reciting Buddha's Name, an example of Otsu-e folk art. . . .
A poem attached to this particular painting reads: "Sage or ordinary
person—there is no difference; / Looking at him you shiver in
your bones, / But listen to the goblin reciting Buddha's name / And
you will smile at the picture on the wall." *(See page 161)*

The Priest Hsien-tzu (c. fourteenth century), by Kao. *(See page 170)*

TWENTY

The Bagworm

Come to my hut
And hear the cry
Of the bagworm.

Minomushi no	Bagworm of
ne wo kiki ni koyo	note hear to come!
kusa no io	grass of hermitage

THE FORM *Ne* means "sound" or "note" as in "note of music." *Wo* puts "note" into the accusative case—"hear the note." *Ni* means "in order to," and the ending *yo* of *koyo* (come) indicates the imperative mood. So the second segment is literally "come to hear the note!" "Hermitage of grass" means "hermitage with a grass roof."

COMMENT This haiku involves a kind of "in" joke, for the

bagworm does not make any sound at all. It just sits in its little bag, gestating and metamorphosing into a moth. Other poets have declared that the voice of the bagworm is ever so thin and pathetic.[1] This idea is similar to an early haiku by Bashō:

> With what voice
> And what song do you sing, spider?
> Autumn wind.

Kumo nanto	Spider with what
oto nanto naku	sound with what voice
aki no kaze	autumn of wind

Though this poem reflects a deep love for all creatures, it has a rather weird feeling that compares interestingly with Bashō's more forthright, later work.

The bagworm has endeared itself to Japanese poets down to to the present. Nakagawa Sōen Rōshi is one such modern poet:

> The place established
> For the bagworm
> Is among the cherry blossoms.

Minomushi no	Bagworm of
tokoro sadameshi	place fixed
hana no naka[2]	blossoms of inside

The little white cocoon hangs there among the cherry flowers, and that is the place that is fixed for it in the scheme of things.

Yosa Buson, another great haiku poet, wrote the following haiku about the bagworm:

> Even the bagworm
> Goes "chi-chi,"
> And the snail?[3]

Minomushi wa	Bagworm:
chichi to mo naku wo	"chichi" even cries
katatsumuri	snail

In the days before pollution and deliberately introduced predators in Hawaii, you could find snails with colored shells in *ohia lehua* trees in the mountains behind Manoa Valley and elsewhere on all the islands of Hawaii. As a boy, I collected them, and a curator at the Bishop Museum told me that people skilled at collecting would listen for their cry—a very tiny sound. Then one day, many years later, I met one of those old-timers, a Hawaiian man, who verified this. He said the snails go "peep-peep." Once you hear that sound, you will always be able to identify it, he said.

Buson didn't know about this and asks: "Well, we know what kind of a sound the bagworm makes. It goes *chi-chi*. What kind of sound does the snail make?" I can tell him. It goes "peep-peep." *Chichi* means "papa" in Japanese, and so the bagworm is the insect of filial piety. You may think this is getting outrageously precious, but haiku is play, after all.

Once I had a genteel argument with my beloved friend Katsuki Sekida about Robert de Ropp's book *The Master Game*.[4] He felt the word "game" was frivolous, and I could not persuade him that "game" and "play" were truly descriptive of our practice. It *is* a game, and one puts oneself totally into it, forgetting the player. On the other hand, the deadly grim student has a hard time with zazen. What did Sōen Rōshi mean when he said that I should handle the koan mu lightly? Muuuuuuuuuuu. Just mu. No thought of taking it seriously.

To return to the sound of no-sound: when Vimalakīrti, great contemporary of the Buddha, became ill, the Buddha sent Manjushrī with 32,000 Bodhisattvas, Arhats, and devas to inquire after his health. Vimalakīrti graciously accommodated them all in his room that measured ten feet by ten feet, and a Dharma battle began. The question was: "What is the Bodhisattva-gate to the Dharma of not-two?" The 32,000

Bodhisattvas, Arhats, and devas gave their opinions. Then Manjushrī said: "In all phenomena, there are no words, no explanations, no presentations, no consciousness; there is freedom from all questions and answers." Finally it was Vimalakīrti's turn. What did the old master say? He did not say anything. He just sat there like the bagworm.[5] Even more silent than the bagworm. He did not even go *chi-chi*. But everybody said they heard quite a lot. You will find Hakuin's portrait of the old master Vimalakīrti sitting there in vivid silence as the frontispiece of D. T. Suzuki's *Manual of Zen Buddhism*.[6]

All of Zen is "in" joke and intimacy, which Bashō expresses in his invitation to come and hear the bagworm. The intimacy that teacher and student feel is the shared experience of hearing Vimalakīrti's thundering silence, together with Manjushrī and 32,000 cohorts.

John Keats knew about the sound of no sound. In his "Ode on a Grecian Urn," he wrote:

> Heard melodies are sweet, but those unheard
> Are sweeter; therefore, ye soft pipes, play on;
> Not to the sensual ear, but more endear'd,
> Pipe to the spirit ditties of no tone.

As R. H. Blyth has pointed out, these lines bear an uncanny resemblance to another of Bashō's haiku:

> I hear the unblown flute
> In shade beneath the trees
> At Suma Temple.[7]

Suma-dera ya	Suma temple!
fukanu fue kiku	unblown flute hear
ko shita yami	tree beneath shade

This is a reference to the tragic execution of the the seventeen-year-old Taira Atsumori in the war between the Taira and Minamoto clans in the twelfth century. Bashō visited Suma Temple, near Osaka, deeply shadowed by old pine trees, and saw there the flute that Atsumori used to play. Like the pipes on the Grecian urn, Atsumori's flute was mute, but Bashō could hear its tones as he paid profound respect to the youthful leader of five hundred years before. Now we today, still another three hundred years later, may hear that same *shakuhachi* if we listen reverently.

Hakuin took an expression from Hsueh-tou Ch'ung-hsien, compiler of *The Blue Cliff Record,* and asked: "What is the sound of a single hand?" This koan has been mistranslated by Western writers as "What is the sound of one hand clapping?" There is no "clapping" in the original. *Seki* is the key word there. It means "one of a pair." What is the sound of one of a pair of hands? "Single hand" is the best translation, but for zazen purposes, it is good just to breathe "one hand" with inhalation and exhalation. I do not recommend this koan for beginners because in my opinion it tends to provoke speculation. However, great masters have used it in the past, and Senzaki Nyogen Sensei told me that it was his first koan when he practiced under Shaku Sōen Rōshi. As Hsueh-tou says: "The sound of a single hand does not come forth and make a sound in vain."[8]

> What is on the radio tonight?
> Who knows?
> Can you turn it on?

TWENTY-ONE

Flower Viewing

Come
To the true flower viewing
Of the life of pilgrimage.

Kusa makura	Grass pillow
makoto no hanami	true of flower viewing
shite mo koyo	do even come

THE FORM   *Kusa makura* is the grass pillow of the pilgrim and becomes an idiom for the life of pilgrimage and poverty. *Hanami* is the idiom for the excursion to see cherry blossoms, and *shite* converts the "flower viewing" into a verb. The *mo* is a particle of emphasis, implying that it would be nice if you would do true flower viewing. Finally, *koyo* is the strong imperative of the verb "to come."

COMMENT   So far as I can determine, this haiku is translated by only one Western scholar, R. H. Blyth.[1] Perhaps other scholars may find it thin and didactic, and so decide to leave it alone. For our purposes, however, it is quite interesting, and not unlike "The Bagworm" in its emphasis upon the essential world.

True flower viewing, the true life of aesthetic enjoyment, is not merely something to be taken up periodically with excursions to groves of cherry trees or in quaint ceremonies in little tea huts with vessels of strange shapes and impressive provenances. It is a certain kind of attitude and life style to which Bashō invites us.

Bashō would smile at pilgrims today. We buy a pack and a sleeping bag from a reputable dealer in mountaineering equipment and set out on an airplane with our gear in the baggage compartment. Then we hike a few hundred feet from the airport to the highway and hitch to our campground. We are like Marie Antoinette, playing at poverty, and few of us are able to do "true flower viewing."

Yasubara Teishitsu, a poet who preceded Bashō by a generation or so, has the following much-admired haiku about flower viewing that contrasts vividly with the spirit of the grass pillow poem:

> This! this!
> I could only say at flowery
> Mount Yoshino.

Kore wa kore wa	"This! this!"
to bakari hana no	only flowers of
Yoshino yama[2]	Yoshino mountain

Japanese to this day are fond of quoting this haiku, and some who should know better ascribe it to Bashō.[3] It too is a poem of pilgrimage, but of a different sort entirely from

143

Bashō's reality. The "Ah!" experience, so dear to Japanese, is epitomized by Teishitsu in connection with the most beautiful flowering trees in Japan at the very place where they are perhaps the most famous—the very place where at cherry-blossom time Bashō could not bring himself to write about the beautiful scene. The "Ah!" was a cliché in this case, a conditioned response rather than a genuine one.

However, at Yoshino, Bashō could address a haiku to his *kasa,* an umbrella-shaped hat worn by farmers and Zen monks:

> I will show you
> Cherry blossoms at Yoshino,
> Cedar-strip *kasa.*

Yoshino nite	Yoshino at
sakura mishō zo	cherry will show!
hinokigasa	cedar *kasa*

The humorous attention he devoted to his hat leads us to conclude that Bashō wished here to show the vanity of the conventional haiku subject and of the conventional "Ah!" experience. He was quite consistent in this avoidance of such conventions, though once, at Matsushima, in spite of himself it seems, he wrote a haiku about the popular but nonetheless remarkable pine-clad islands. This lapse was nothing, however, compared to the ultimate in elegant vacuity that is often blamed on Bashō: *Matsushima ya | ā Matsushima ya | Matsushima ya.* It is so bald that it does not need translating.[4]

One of Bashō's pilgrimages was to the village of Sarashina, northwest of Tokyo in present Nagano Prefecture. Sarashina is reputed to be the best place in Japan to view the full moon of autumn. It was not in Bashō to write a haiku about the beauty of the moon and its reflection in the rice paddies. However, he wrote a fine poem about horse chestnuts that echoes his "Flower Viewing" haiku:

Horse chestnuts
Will be my presents
To people of the world.

Kiso no tochi	Kiso of horse chestnuts
ukiyo no hito no	floating world of people of
miyage kana	presents!

As I indicated earlier, ukiyo is the "floating world" of samsāra, and more specifically here, the world of periodic excursions into aesthetics where one goes "Ah! Ah!" at a given circumstance because that is the established, elegant exclamation for such a time and place. For people of that world, rare and lovely things are valued, and a common object like a horse chestnut is passed over as having no interest. But really, the horse chestnut is an extraordinary object, as every child would know.

Miyage, or more commonly *omiyage,* is an ancient Japanese word that means literally "aboriginal product." An omiyage from Hawaii might be a koa bowl. It is another Japanese word, *kinen,* that means "souvenir" or "remembrance." It has always been important for the traveler about Japan to bring home omiyage to his friends and relatives—not souvenirs, but products of regional crafts in an otherwise homogeneous culture. Instead of something elegant, Bashō proposes horse chestnuts for his worldly friends. A good lesson for them, he seems to be saying. Here is the true miyage.

In Zen, the old worthies knew about flower viewing and miyage. A monk asked Yun-men: "What is Buddha?" Yun-men said: "*Kan shih chueh* [dried shit stick]!"[5] The dried shit stick was a piece of wood used just as our ancestors used a corncob in their outhouses. A dried-up old stick that had been used for such a purpose might be the ultimate in useless objects from a worldly point of view. In Yun-men's time, "dried shit stick" was also an epithet, and beyond this, there is the koan content of his encounter with the monk to consider.

145

In any case, the elegance of Buddha is brought down to the earth of the earth, to the fundamentals of pilgrimage, grass pillow, and horse chestnut. I am reminded of Robert Louis Stevenson's fable ''The Poor Thing,'' in which the fisherman stands in the marketplace with an old horseshoe in his creel for sale. With it he wins the daughter of the earl for his wife.[6] With a dried shit stick, with a single horse chestnut, we discover the true blessedness of poverty.

Do not suppose this blessedness is simply a matter of possessing ordinary things rather than elaborate things. Bashō is offering a hint, as Jesus did with his warning that it is easier for a camel to pass through the eye of a needle than for a rich man to enter the kingdom of heaven. There are plenty of poor men and women who are stuck in the ordinary world of precious and useless, and who have no realization of heaven or the lotus land.

The rock garden of Ryōan-ji temple in Kyoto is like the horse chestnut of Bashō. It is just an expanse of sand interspersed with a few stones and surrounded by a mud wall. But nowadays I hear there are hordes of visitors, a recorded commentary over loudspeakers, and a souvenir store, all taken up with the precious nature of (famous) plain beauty.

> Little white maggots
> In fermenting night soil
> Steam with Buddhahood.

TWENTY-TWO

Birds Crying

Departing spring!
Birds crying;
Tears in the eyes of fish.

Yuku haru ya	Departing spring!
tori naki uo no	birds cry fish of
me wa namida	eyes: tears

THE FORM   The setting is established first, marked off by the cutting word *ya*. Departing spring is the time just before the beginning of summer—the flowering trees have passed and the rainy season is about to start. In the second segment, there is one complete clause, "Birds cry," and the beginning of a second clause, "In the eyes of fish: tears."

COMMENT   Most translators render *naki* as "weep," but this is incorrect. Its homonym means "weep," and so this carries through as an overtone, but the ideograph Bashō used refers to the cry of any animal, with reference derived from context. Understanding this point clearly is essential to understanding the poem. The Japanese scholar Katō Shūkō explicates: "Spring is about to pass away, and even unfeeling birds cry with indefinable melancholy, and tears may be seen in the eyes of fish. The parting of Bashō from people who see him off is thus summed up and concealed."[1]

Bashō is here setting off on his great journey to the northern parts of Japan, which he later commemorated in *The Narrow Way Within*. It was the second haiku of the trip, written when he was seen off by his friends. Everyone wept at his departure, knowing the hardship of his proposed journey and the possibility that they might be separating forever.

Fumiko Fujikawa suggests that Bashō is here echoing the poem "Spring—The Long View" by Tu Fu, Bashō's favorite Chinese poet.[2] The pertinent part of this poem runs:

> Though the nation is shattered
> Its hills and streams remain;
> It is spring [again] in the cities;
> Grasses and trees are luxuriant.
> Overwhelmed by changes of time,
> Flowers seem to shed tears;
> Lamenting my separation [from family]
> Birds seem to be moved.[3]

I have used Professor Fujikawa's translation here. I am not a scholar of Chinese and may have missed the nuances which she translates as "seem." My impression is that Tu Fu says plainly that flowers weep and birds lament.

Anyway, she comments: "Although Bashō is in quite a different situation than Tu Fu and Bashō's mood in parting from his friends was not burdened by Tu Fu's fear and uneasiness, he nevertheless uses images similar to those of the Chinese poet. Bashō's weeping birds, for example, and his fish with tear-laden eyes are but variations of Tu Fu's lamenting birds and tear-shedding flowers.''[4]

I agree that the images were similar, and that the mood and circumstances were different. Indeed, if Bashō used "Spring—The Long View" for inspiration—and this seems very likely—it was simply to pick out the idea of birds and other elements of nature expressing sadness, and to use this idea with quite a different meaning.

Tu Fu deplores the tragic condition of his country in the throes of civil war, and he worries about possibly not seeing his family again. By spelling out these causal factors, Tu Fu puts the conceits of flowers weeping and birds feeling sad into the dimension of human action and reaction.

Bashō is not saying that birds cry sadly and tears well in the eyes of the fish because he, Bashō, is parting from his friends. He is saying that spring itself is departing; there are tears in the eyes of birds and fish, and (not expressed, but surely implied) all other creatures. Even in seventeen syllables, Bashō could have included something about saying farewell to his friends, if he had wanted to, and the human schema of Tu Fu would have been maintained. Instead, Bashō himself disappears, and there is just weeping. This is the universality of the particular, the experience that "When I am sad, the whole universe is sad; when I am glad, the whole universe is glad," to use Yamada Kōun Rōshi's words. Notice the use of "when" here, not "because"—concurrence, not consequence.

On the same pilgrimage, a few months later, Bashō composed a memorial verse for the young poet Isshō:

> Shake, oh grave;
> My wailing voice
> Is the autumn wind.

Tsuka mo ugoke	Grave move
waga naku koe wa	my weeping voice:
aki no kaze	autumn of wind

Ugoke at the end of the first segment is in the imperative mood. It means literally "move, quake, sway, shake." There is a touch of the pathetic fallacy in this first portion of the poem, as the inanimate grave is commanded to shake with sorrow, even as the poet is shaking. However, in the last two parts we have a clear expression of cosmic lament. The poet and the cosmic sangha are one. The whole universe wails with Bashō, as Bashō.

You may feel that there is little difference between this approach and that of Tu Fu. Tu Fu also sees the universality of his own emotion. Indeed, this is probably what Bashō appreciated when taking images of the earlier poet for his own. However, when Bashō presents his emotions, there is no feeling of "seem." His journal carries the context of his lament of Isshō and of the birds crying, but the haiku themselves are completely pure, with no conceptual element at all.

When Tu Fu says that the country is in distress and that *therefore* the flowers are weeping, he is using a conceit on the level of simile, and the words "as though" and "seem" come to mind, as they do for Professor Fujikawa. There is consequence, not concurrence. Human chauvinism prompts a conceptual suspension of reality, and we are projected into an imaginary world where flowers and birds behave like people.

Bashō's world of poetry is the world of experience, not intellectual association. The simile of "as though" is supplanted by the metaphor of flowing unity. Bashō disappears, and the season itself is going; the birds and fish themselves are sad. The autumn wind becomes his wailing voice. This is the nature of deepest poetry, of deepest religious insight. "Heaven and earth and I are of the same root. All things and I are one."[5]

This expression of unity in all things, manifested in the world of karma, is presented over and over in Bashō's haiku.

Here is another verse from *The Narrow Way Within,* one of
the deepest of all:

> Summer grasses!
> The imprint of dreams
> Of warriors.

Natsugusa ya	Summer grasses!
tsuwamonodomo ga	warriors of
yume no ato	dreams of remains

Ato is a very interesting Japanese word. With the ideograph
Bashō used here, it means "mark, print, impression," and it
is part of such idioms as "footprint" or "toothmark." By
extension, it has many possible implications, depending on the
context: one of these is "remains" or "ruins," as in "ruins
of a temple."

Bashō was visiting the ruins of Takadate Castle at Hiraizumi,
where a historic battle was fought in the civil war of the late
twelfth century. It was a terrible tragedy, ending with the
great general Yoshitsune committing suicide after killing his
wife and children.

Professor Fujikawa suggests that the image of grasses after
the war was also lifted from Tu Fu's poem "Spring—The
Long View":

> Though the nation is shattered
> Its hills and streams remain;
> It is spring [again] in the cities;
> Grasses and trees are luxuriant.

She comments: "Tu Fu, the social poet, sees order in
political terms, while the mystically-minded Bashō sees in
nature the eternity of the cosmic order."[6] Tu Fu is lamenting
the destruction of his society, and noting with irony that
grasses and trees flourish despite the ruination. Bashō is saying,

with his vivid use of the word *ato,* that the grasses are the outcome of the terrible battle at Hiraizumi. That battle was a dream of warriors, and here the grasses flourish as the ruins of that dream.

The social world of rebellion and the natural world of trees and grasses were for Tu Fu two separate worlds, one persisting despite the other. But for Bashō, as we have seen in his other haiku ("You are the butterfly / And I the dreaming heart / Of Chuang-tzu"), it is all a dream, the movement of form to form, now high drama and fiercest violence, now grasses, now Bashō, now you and I.

This is not necessarily the world of the recluse. Once, in discussing the danger of nuclear weapons with Katsuki Sekida, I expressed my feelings of profound dismay and fear. He said: "Well, of course the Rings of Saturn must have come from a great explosion." I acknowledge this cosmic view, as I resist the construction of the Trident nuclear submarine.

> Cardinals sing at Punchbowl
> Cemetery the silence
> Of my parents.

TWENTY-THREE

Miming

With my fan
I mime drinking sakè—
Falling cherry blossoms.

Ogi nite   Fan with
sakè kumu kage ya   sakè drink mime!
chiru sakura   falling cherry

THE FORM   This haiku hinges at the end of the second segment with the cutting word *ya*, which separates the action of
the first two parts from the setting in the last part. *Ya* is
again a particle of anticipation, for it is only with a statement
of the falling cherry petals that the action of drinking sakè with
a fan becomes meaningful. Sakè is rice wine, virtually the only
alcoholic beverage known in Japan during Bashō's time.

COMMENT Cherry-blossom time is traditionally the occasion for a sakè party under the trees, but for Bashō, the mime of drinking with a fan was appropriate. The setting of petals swirling down in the cool spring wind is altogether dreamlike, taking the poet out of the world of "certain certainties" and placing him in the realm of a play.

Drinking with the fan is a pantomime found both in Noh drama and in *kyōgen,* the comical reflex of Noh. In kyōgen, drunkenness is commonly a hilarious theme. The actor spreads his fan, lifts it to his lips, tips his head back, and drinks. It is an elegant conceit, and we have the sense that wine is actually draining off the folds of the decorated paper.

Bashō wrote this haiku when he was forty-four years old, while on pilgrimage in the Kansai area, somewhere around Osaka perhaps. It is not given much notice in Japanese critical literature, and many translators, including Blyth and Miyamori, ignore it altogether. For our purposes, however, it is quite interesting.

How is it possible to drink with a fan? The philistine will say it is not possible. Nobuyuki Yuasa renders the poem:

> Using my fan
> For a cup
> I pretend to drink
> Under the scattering cherry.[1]

Bashō is not pretending, he is miming, and this can be carried a step further. Marcel Marceau is not a mime. He *is* that kite-flyer, and, sitting there under the falling petals, Bashō is actually drinking wine. He is free of bottles, as Marceau is free of string. He is the act itself.

Analytically, we may say that Marceau mimes and that Bashō mimes the mime of the Noh actor. So in that sense, Bashō is freer than Marceau. He is free of bottles and of Noh apparatus too—costumes, music, stage, audience, and the rest.

There is another story about freedom. Some time ago at

Koko An, we played the game of *shōsan*. This is a way of opening up the dokusan procedure—people come forward for public, rather than private, confrontation with the rōshi. This time Chen Yu-hsi came forward and began his presentation with the famous haiku by Moritake: "The fallen flower / Has returned to the branch; / No, it was a butterfly."[2]

Then he said: "Ten years ago I met you and did zazen at this training center. Then for a long time I thought I could never come back. Now, like a fallen flower, I have returned to the branch. How is this possible?"

I said: "In a dream, all things are possible."

This story is made especially poignant when we understand that Chen Yu-hsi was forcibly returned to the Republic of China from Japan, where he had been studying on a grant from the East-West Center of the University of Hawaii. He was imprisoned in Taiwan for four years, then severely restricted for another four years before diplomatic pressure from the United States opened the way for him to return to Hawaii and resume his studies.

With empty hands, Marcel Marceau dreams he flies a kite. Bashō dreams he is a Noh player, miming with a fan. In a dream fulfilled, Chen Yu-hsi dreams he does zazen at Koko An. Is Chen Yu-hsi a Zen student at Koko An who dreamt he was a prisoner, or a prisoner who is dreaming that he is sitting here with us?

At the Maui Zendo, we have a memento of Yamamoto Gempō Rōshi hanging above the door to our commons room. It is his calligraphy of the ideograph "dream," carved on a block of wood by the artist Shin Segawa. He inscribed that ideograph when he was ninety-two years old. Why should a great Zen master write "dream" as a memento for his descendants?

Any child can show you. When I go to the Peahi Nursery School and read a story to the children, we have fun after the story, acting it out. One child turns into a tree. Another turns into a blackberry bush. Another turns into a rabbit. Still another becomes a crotchety old man named Mr.

MacGregor. And how the fur flies! In a dream, all such things are possible.

Now you are a student, now a pedestrian, now a spouse or lover, now a gardener, and so on—now a butterfly, now a prisoner, now a doctoral candidate. However, even as a prisoner, when you stand up, there is only that standing up. You are just the act of standing. Nothing is sticking to it, and that standing up is independent of everything in the whole universe.

On the other hand, if you think of being a student as you turn the page and look up unfamiliar words, then you are maundering in a limbo where no action is real and no action can be fulfilled. Just turn the page. Just look up the words. As a pedestrian, just walk, just watch the trees, sky, and passing cars. This is not mere concentration. It is the freedom from self-concern that is true devotion. Devotion is the quality of your dream.

Thich Nhat Hanh says: "Every act is a rite. Does the word 'rite' seem too solemn? I use that word in order to jolt you into the realization of the life-and-death matter of awareness."[3]

Some people are very suspicious of ceremony—the rite of a Noh drama under the cherry trees, the rite of flying a kite without a string, the rite of Peter Rabbit, the rite of zazen in a prison, or in a conventional dōjō—but such suspicion is an unwillingness to invest the self, the worst prison of all. What is more free than the transformation of Chuang-tzu to a butterfly and back, of a Zen teacher to a gardener, of a prisoner to a graduate student? When each act is a rite, each role is sacred. There is nothing to fear, nothing to protect, and self-centeredness has vanished completely.

"I'm a fire engine!" shouts the child, "RRRrrr!" We hold ears and smile patronizingly, imprisoned in our plans for the future and our memories of the past. Another time, we perhaps scold the child for dawdling over breakfast, when actually she is noticing carefully the difference each bite makes upon a brown island of cereal in a sea of white milk.

Bashō under the scattering petals played at being a Noh actor in a dream of pink and white motion. The more conventional celebrant drinks in order to get drunk, just as the usual way of washing the dishes is to wash them in order to make them clean.[4] All Zen founders caution us about the vanity of doing "in order to." Nan-yueh Huai-jang warned that if you do zazen in order to become a Buddha, you will never become one.[5]

Life is a dream, as the *Diamond Sutra* says. In the season of Bon, the Japanese festival of the dead, we dream that the dead come back and dance with the living. For this purpose, they are escorted from the graveyard with a special ceremony, and then at the end of the season they are escorted back. In the Bon dances, some people dance with towels over their faces, representing the dead. The facts of debit and credit fade before this reality.

A monk asked Yang-shan Hui-chi: "Your Reverence, do you know ideographs or not?"

Yang-shan said: "As my profession requires."

The monk immediately turned around once to the right and asked: "What ideograph is that?" Yang-shan drew the ideograph for "ten" (similar to a Greek cross) on the earth.

The monk turned himself around once to the left and said: "What ideograph is that?" Yang-shan modified the "ten" into a swastika.

The monk drew a circle in the air, and lifted his two palms like Asura holding the sun and moon, and said: "What ideograph is that?" Yang-shan promptly drew a circle enclosing the swastika.

The monk at once represented the vigor of a guardian deity. Yang-shan said: "Good, good. Keep it with care."[6]

What is more vivid than these old-timers dancing around, drawing ideographs and circles on the ground, miming angels and guardians, fallen away completely in the drama of Dharma combat? What is more vivid than the child who has turned into Peter Rabbit, or Bashō as a Noh player knocking back wine with his fan? What is more vivid than the mother who becomes a French teacher, devoting herself to conjugating irregular verbs?

In a dream at night, we are caught up in just that dream, flitting and fluttering around. It is in just such total awareness that body and mind fall away as mu, as one's original face before the Buddha appeared in the world. It is in the dimension of evolution, of present means toward future ends, of doing in order to, that staleness, cynicism, and boredom are so overwhelming.

> Are you digging to China?
> No, dummy!
> That's Botswana down there!

TWENTY-FOUR

The Beginning of Culture

The beginning of culture!
Rice-planting songs
In the innermost part of the country.

Fūryū no	Culture of
hajime ya oku no	beginning! inner
ta ue uta	rice field planting song

THE FORM *Fūryū* is an idiom translated as "culture, elegance, refinement." *Fū* literally means "wind" and is used here in the way we use the word "air" to mean manner, tone, or style. *Ryū* means "flow," as in "flow of a stream," and, by extension, "tradition." *Fūryū* is an important term in Bashō's own critical writing and in contemporary Japanese criticism of art and literature.

COMMENT   The traditional way to plant rice in Japan is to flood the small fields and then to plant seedlings in the mud. On levees two foremen squat, holding a line taut between them across a field. Women wading in the mud stand in a row behind the line, holding seedlings in their hands. Then, with a song that is accompanied by flutes and drums, they bend over and plant the seedlings in line with the string. A leader holds a ceremonial staff and sings the verses, while the women and other men sing the chorus as they work. The song progresses, the line moves back, and the process is repeated until the field is completely planted. Looking down a line of seedlings is like sighting through a miniature forest that has been set out with a transit. Each little plant is equidistant from those on each side of it, and all the available space is completely utilized. I watched farmers planting rice in this way in Sawaji, near Ryūtaku monastery, many years ago.

At that time, I did not know that Japanese folklore relates the fecundity of the women planters to the richness of the soil.[1] Like Bashō, I was particularly impressed with the lovely, antique quality of their songs. Years later, on vacation at an inn near Numazu, my wife Anne and I wakened to hear fishermen far out in the bay singing as they hauled in their nets—a beautiful beginning for our day.

Bashō places work songs at the source of culture. Perhaps it would be difficult to prove such a thing historically, but certainly they communicate that source, and this, I think, is what Bashō felt.

Fūryū not only may mean "elegance," it is itself an elegant word, and you will not find it elsewhere in Bashō's haiku, just as you will not find the other elegant terms of Japanese literary criticism—shibui (refined), hosomi (delicate), and the like—in his poems. However, his interpretation of elegance is the heart of his tao.

Hanami, or cherry-blossom viewing, was for Bashō most truly realized in a life of humble pilgrimage. Refined social customs were best fulfilled in such ways as presenting horse chestnuts to friends. Yet it was not merely the choice of the commonplace as elegant. We must look closely at Bashō's intention. For him it was the "natural staff without artificial work" that was truly elegant.[2] "Old" and "origin" were words of special significance to him, as they are to students of Zen.

Once, as a young Zen student, I visited Sen no Rikyū's own tea hut in Kyoto with Nakagawa Sōen Rōshi. We had no utensils with us, so we mimed the ceremony. As I drank the tea of no-taste, the Rōshi asked me: "How old is that bowl?"

I said: "It is so old, I cannot remember its age." Though the Rōshi praised my answer, I had no understanding of its significance then. It is with the old that we touch the timeless, the dimension that is neither old nor new.

Bashō felt this timelessness on hearing the rice planting songs, and he felt it in folk art as well as in folk music:

> With what Buddha
> Did Otsu-e painting
> Begin?

Otsu-e no	Otsu pictures of
fude no hajime wa	brush of beginning:
nani-botoke	what Buddha

Otsu-e takes its name from a place near Kyoto that has produced Buddhist and other folk art from earliest times. "What Buddha is the source of that?" Bashō asks, a true koan that takes us back not only in time but into ourselves, where all beings by nature are Buddha. We find our own origins in the ancient arts.

I think the true cause of distress—in Japan, in the United States, and everywhere—over commercialization and so-called development lies in the sense of losing the ancient. Loss of the ancient means loss of the realization of the timeless in the

161

present time, whenever an old tree is cut, whenever an old landmark is razed.

> The village is old;
> No house
> Without its persimmon tree.

Sato furite	Village is old
kaki no ki motanu	persimmon of tree without
ie mo nashi	house even none

"Old village" is an idiom that strikes a deep chord in all Japanese, even today. It refers to the ancestral home, perhaps the place the individual was actually born, or perhaps not, but in any case the place of one's personal roots. When such places are destroyed, the roots of the individual wither. Here Bashō comes across a truly ancient village, each house with its own full-grown persimmon tree. Again, with an experience of the ancient, he is in touch with the timeless.

Currently one hears a lot of nonsense about nonattachment to things. We should be free of the need for particular forms and experiences, some people say. However, the human being is a sentient being. It is through the senses that we reach no seeing, no hearing, no feeling, and so on. Moreover, the sense experience that is repeated from ancient days as ritual can evoke the one who is not born and does not die.

> A village where no temple bell sounds—
> What do they do?
> Twilight in spring.

Kane tsukanu	Bell not rung
mura wa nani wo ka	village: what?
haru no kure	spring of evening

Bashō is asking, where there is no temple bell at evening, how can people function? How indeed? When we have no reminders of our timeless nature, there is no possibility of finding our way. Even a humanist liberal who deliberately avoids ritual as a denial of personal freedom is moved when the great temple bell is struck. The abyss of that sound is the great void, and anyone who hears will be at least momentarily confirmed. Bashō is saying that a village without that profound means to resonate the heart-minds of its householders is lost. What can people do? They are no longer in touch.

When students weep in the dōjō, they sometimes worry about it and come to me afterwards to ask why zazen should prompt such a reaction. Depending upon circumstances, I will sometimes point out that weeping, like laughing, is a symptom of being in touch with one's self. It is not something one should criticize, unless it becomes a kind of indulgence. Occasionally an outburst of weeping is kenshō itself.

Being in touch means that ordinary self-preoccupation has fallen away. There is no point of reference, as a student once remarked to me. There is just the act, just the sense. Just standing up, just hearing the bell.

But we need skillful means. The very word *sesshin,* which we translate as "retreat" or "seclusion," means, in part, "to touch the mind." Without training, the experience is not likely to take root. Without his training, Bashō's encounters with folk music, folk art, the old village, and the village without a temple bell would have had no import. Truly to touch the mind we need a life designed to touch it. That is the Buddha-tao.

Bashō himself wrote the best verse to end this chapter:

> Though in Kyoto,
> I long for Kyoto
> At the song of the cuckoo.

Kyō nite mo	Kyoto in even
Kyō natsukashi ya	Kyoto long for!
hototogisu	cuckoo.

163

TWENTY-FIVE

The Priest and Chrysanthemum Flowers

Drinking his morning tea
The priest is peaceful—
Chrysanthemum flowers.

Asa cha nomu	Morning tea drinks
sō shizuka nari	priest peaceful is
kiku no hana	chrysanthemum of flowers

THE FORM   The first two segments of this poem are in apposition to the third. The peace of the priest drinking his morning tea is the peace of the chrysanthemums.

COMMENT   There are several words Bashō might have used to mean "priest." The term *bonzō*, literally "Buddhist priest," may have been current in Bashō's time, but it is rarely heard today. It was apparently the term taken by Francis Xavier and Latinized, whence we get our English word "bonze."[1] Similar words are *bōzu* and *bōsan,* literally "master of a temple," which are pejorative except when used informally by priests among themselves. *Unsui* is an elegant term meaning "cloud and water," and refers to monks in training, usually young fellows at a monastery. *Oshō* is a title meaning "honored father," and it projects a personal quality that is missing from *unsui.* There are many other terms meaning "priest," some of them very fanciful. The female form is *ni,* meaning "Buddhist nun," and is a title used after a name. *Ama* is the usual term for "Buddhist nun" when a specific name is not used.

Bashō uses the word *sō* to mean "priest." *Sō* is the word that translates sangha, the third of the Three Treasures of Buddhism, and its usage to mean "priest" echoes the old interpretation of the sangha as the community of ordained disciples who gathered about the Buddha. Bashō presents the person with black robes and shaved head as a treasure of Buddha nature.

Sō could be male or female. The dress is precisely the same for both. Very young unsui and very young ama are sometimes mistaken for each other, as occasionally are very old oshō and very old ama. Statistically, however, the ama are a tiny minority, and I have the feeling that Bashō, with his eye for the particular and the unique, would have come up with a poem to fit such uniqueness if the priest had been a woman.

To return to the haiku, tea drinking is traditionally an act of peace, and I think Bashō is saying the priest settles into his original place of peace as he drinks his tea. The priest truly manifests as priest as he drinks his tea.

The chrysanthemum is the symbol of the imperial house of Japan and is idealized as the symbol of purity. The presence of chrysanthemums in apposition to the priest reinforces the quality of aesthetic purity in his act of drinking tea.

Here is another poem by Bashō on chrysanthemums:

White chrysanthemums;
Not a speck of dust
To meet the eye.

Shiragiku no	White chrysanthemums of
me ni tatete miru	eye to meet see
chiri mo nashi	dust even none

For Zen students, this is reminiscent of the expression often used by their teachers: "Not a bit of cloud in the empty sky meets my eyes."[2] It is *shūnyatā,* the void, experienced at the deepest human level.

Purity should be understood as an attitude that rises from realization of that which is neither stained nor pure. It is an attitude and, I hope, not a fixation. Purity does not necessarily mean celibacy, for example, though celibacy can be extremely rewarding for the person who has truly sublimated sex. Most people can sublimate sex for a while, say for a period of residence at a training center, but eventually there may be a problem. The self may resist the self in maintaining an artificial standard, to no good end.

Purity and serenity in the environment inspire the realization of essential purity and serenity within. The Buddha on the altar, the neatness and cleanness of the dōjō, flowers, pictures, incense, and other adjuncts of our practice all contribute to this realization. The priest personifies purity and serenity with his cleanly shaved head, his neatly pressed robes, and his dignified demeanor.

Some people idealize the priest as a person who has evolved to a high level of spirituality that the benighted lay person cannot expect to achieve in this life or even the next, but may, with diligent effort, attain after many lives. Others find no fundamental separation between clerical and lay, and find the priest expressive of the inner life of all humanity. I prefer the latter view.

The priest endeavors to express inner realization and serenity in the context of temple life. The lay person endeavors to express inner realization and serenity in the context of the home and job—as homemaker, schoolteacher, attorney, or whatever. Sometimes there are in-between categories, like haiku poets of Bashō's day who wore Zen Buddhist robes but entered temples only as visitors.

Beyond purity, serenity, and a dignified demeanor, the aesthetic dimension is essential to true practice:

> The fragrance of chrysanthemums
> At Nara:
> Many ancient Buddhas.

Kiku no ka ya	Chrysanthemum of fragrance!
Nara ni wa furuki	Nara at: ancient
hotoke-tachi	Buddhas

This poem really deserves its own chapter, for it is one of the most resonant of all Japanese haiku. In the faint fragrance of chrysanthemums, Nara emerges with its many old Buddhas, its many ancient Buddhist images.

The Japan of Buddhism, the Japan of Bashō's heart, has its source in the city of Nara, the first historical capital, the first Buddhist center in the country. The chrysanthemums as a symbol of Japan and purity are here expressive of the Buddhist archetypes in Nara, deeply endeared to the Japanese people through many centuries of worship. *Furuki* means "ancient," —not merely very old, but timeless.

In one of the most important koans of Zen study, Pai-chang cremates the body of a dead fox in a ceremony established for funerals of dead priests.[3] In Asia, as in the West, the fox symbolizes all that is dishonest and tricky in human character, while the priest symbolizes full and complete realization and virtue. Yamada Kōun Rōshi cited to me Hakuin's comment on this incident, wherein Hakuin, a thousand years afterwards, denounces Pai-chang for confusing such disparate archetypes.[4] Was Hakuin being ironical? Pai-chang had an important purpose in performing that ceremony. That fire of cremation was expressive of his realization of the true nature of the priest, the true nature of the fox, and the true nature of you and me. Drinking tea or coffee, standing up or sitting down, there is not a speck of dust to be seen.

> The great kalpa fire
> Annihilates the Pope
> And Miss Puss, our cat.

TWENTY-SIX

Net of The Law

The whitebait!
They open black eyes
To the net of the law.

Shirauo ya	Whitebait!
kuroki me wo aku	black eyes open
nori no ami	law of net

THE FORM   The *ya* at the end of the first segment is again a cutting word that sets off "whitebait," as though to say: "Ah, the whitebait!" It also anticipates the comment carried in the next two lines. *Nori* is the Japanese pronunciation of the ideograph that means "law" in the secular sense and "Dharma" in Buddhism.

COMMENT   This is one of Bashō's few haiku that refer directly to Zen Buddhism. It carries the title "Inscription over a Picture of Kensu." Kensu is the Japanese pronunciation of Hsien-tzu, a T'ang-period figure whose story may be found in the *Ch'uan Teng Lu* (Transmission of the Lamp), a Sung-period history of Zen: "As to the Priest Hsien-tzu of Ching-Tiao, we do not know anything about his origins. The record that remains is very strange. He had no fixed place of abode. After receiving transmission of mind from Tung-shan Liang-chieh, he lived as a layman at the River Min. He did not cultivate Dharma devices, and he did not follow conventional modes of behavior. Each day, along the bank of the river, he set about catching prawns."[1] Katō Shūkō comments: "So instead of assembling people and preaching the Dharma, he took up his net and captured prawn beings with great energy."[2]

The *Transmission of the Lamp* continues: "When it got dark, he made his bed in the paper money at the White Horse Mausoleum of Tung-Shan. The residents thereabouts called him Father Prawn."[3] All money in old China was made of metal of one kind or another. Paper money was symbolic material that was burned at funerals to supply the dead with finances needed in the next world. We may suppose that the White Horse Mausoleum had a storeroom full of paper money for such a purpose—a very comfortable place for an old bum like Hsien-tzu to sleep.

It is popularly said that Hsien-tzu was forced to fish for prawns as a layman because the emperor of his time closed down Buddhist temples and turned out the monks and nuns to fend for themselves in the world. It is true that Hsien-tzu lived at about the period when Buddhism was banned, but this aspect is not mentioned in the *Transmission of the Lamp* at all. It seems that Hsien-tzu chose to live by the river as a prawn fisherman quite on his own.

With the freedom of a renku poet, Bashō moves from the usual image of Hsien-tzu, standing there beside the river and holding up a large prawn with evident delight, to that of the whitebait: from fisherman to prey. Katō Shūkō comments: "The eyes of the whitebait are especially black and refreshing, so we may understand that Bashō used whitebait rather than prawns as a matter of poetical preference."[4] This would be one of the renku-like links between the haiku and the picture. Another is the "net of the law," which captures prawns, whitebait, and us all.

Law is not a very popular subject in poetry, but Bashō uses it with its Buddhist implication of Dharma in other haiku as well as this one. Dharma has three meanings: the law of karma; phenomena or things; and the teachings of Buddhism. The law of karma is the way things are; cause leads to effect, which in turn leads to further effects in all directions through endless dimensions. Phenomena are the form of karma; you and I and the Buddha on the altar and the window behind it and Hsientzu's net are all phenomena, things in flux created from past events and creating new events. Finally, the teachings of the Buddha and his successors are expressions of the way things are, presentations of universal tao. These three meanings are really three aspects of one meaning.

Whitebait, of which one variety is called sprats, are small silvery fish, an inch or so long. Their eyes are large in proportion to their size, but even so, in relation to the eyes of the human observer, they are very tiny. The passion of Bashō was his focus upon humble creatures. He presents the luminous depths of black eyes of the whitebait, opening calmly to the net of the way things are.

A traditional koan that Yasutani Hakuun Rōshi liked to use is "The Dry Well." Suppose that you are at the bottom of a dry well, a hundred feet deep. The sides are of completely smooth rock. What do you do?[5] Well, that is only one example. Actually, you are in extremity all day long. How do you handle it?

We can all learn from the whitebait. Whitman wrote:

I think I could turn and live with the animals,
  they are so placid and self-contained,
I stand and look at them long and long.
They do not sweat and whine about their condition,
They do not lie awake in the dark and weep for
  their sins.[6]

Perhaps Whitman is a little heavy in making his point. I
prefer Bashō. The whitebait open black eyes to the net of the
law, as does the octopus:

> Octopus jar!
> Evanescent dreams;
> The summer moon.

Takotsubo ya	Octopus jar!
hakanaki yume wo	evanescent dreams
natsu no tsuki	summer of moon

The postposition *wo* at the end of the second segment indicates that the preceding words are the object of a verb. However, the verb "see" is omitted. In the West, one has a dream.
In the East, one sees it. The subject of the missing verb, too, is
missing. Perhaps it is the octopus itself, dreaming away in the
trap it has crawled into so comfortably. Perhaps it is Bashō,
musing in the fishing boat under the bright summer moon. Perhaps it is life itself. There is Bashō, sitting in a boat moored
in Akashi Bay with fishermen companions, musing over the
octopus musing in its jar. Is there anything outside that dream?
  Of all creatures, I suppose the octopus is one of the most
difficult to identify with, but not for Bashō. Notice how deli-
cately he handles his topic. The idea that the octopus has a
dream, or is a dream, is preposterous and amusing, but he
expresses it without saying it explicitly, and that saves the
poem from sentimentality.
  Black is the expression for night, for the essential world of

172

no discrimination. We open our own black eyes to the net of the law, not just of cause and effect, but of Indra too, in which every point is a jewel that perfectly reflects every other point. The black eyes that Bashō saw are opening all around us, and the octopus moves calmly, awaiting it knows not what.

> On the cattle truck
> Shifting with bumps and curves,
> Eyes turning, heads lifting.

Glossary of Selected Terms

Arhat: enlightened hermit; the ideal of the Theravada Buddhist tradition.

bodhi tree: bo or pipal tree *(Ficus religiosa)*; the tree beneath which the Buddha sat when he realized essential nature.

Bodhisattva: enlightened being; a member of the Buddhist pantheon; one who acts wisely without self-consciousness.

Bon: (Japanese), festival of the dead; festival of lanterns.

Bosatsu: (Japanese), Bodhisattva.

Dharma: the law of cause and effect; phenomena or things; Buddhist doctrine.

dokusan: (Japanese), to go alone with devotion; personal interview with the rōshi.

dōjō: (Japanese), the ground on which the Buddha sat when he was enlightened; a meditation hall (from the Sanskrit *bodhimanda,* spot or place of enlightenment).

haikai: (Japanese), haiku; also used to mean *renku.*

hokku: (Japanese), verse that presents; the first line of a *renku.*

Kanzeon: (Japanese), a Bodhisattva who perceives sounds (of suffering) in the world; also Kannon (Japanese) and Kuanyin (Chinese).

kasa: (Japanese), an umbrella-shaped hat, usually woven of bamboo or sedge.

katsu: (Japanese), a shouted exclamation used to punctuate a Zen discourse.

kenshō: (Japanese), to see into essential nature; realization experience; religious experience.

kinhin: (Japanese), the sutra that is walked; a formal walk between periods of *zazen*.

koan: an existential matter to be made clear. See *mu*.

kotatsu: (Japanese), a foot warmer with a quilt cover over it.

kyōgen: (Japanese), a play; a curtain raiser or interlude during Noh performances.

makyō: (Japanese), mysterious vision; a kind of religious experience usually involving vision or a sense of bodily distortion.

miyage or *omiyage*: (Japanese), aboriginal product; product of a place; a present brought from and representative of a particular place.

mu: (Japanese), no or nothingness (but not to be taken literally when used as a koan); Case One of the *Wu Men Kuan* (*Jap.*, Mumonkan; *Eng.*, The Gateless Barrier); usually the first koan for a Zen student.

prajnā: enlightenment; the actual state of all things.

renku: (Japanese), linked verses, with associations from culture, history, and nature forming the links.

rimpoche: a Tibetan Buddhist master.

rōshi: (Japanese), venerable teacher.

samādhi: absorption; concentration.

samsāra: see *ukiyo*.

sangha: group; Buddhist fellowship; fellowship of all beings.

satori: prajnā; *kenshō*.

senryū: (Japanese), eighteenth-century Japanese humanistic and satirical verses; lit., River Willow, pseudonym of the originator.

sesshin: (Japanese), to touch the mind; to convey or receive the mind; the Zen retreat of from three to seven days.

shakuhachi: (Japanese), a five-holed flute.

shibui: (Japanese), astringent; refined.

shōsan: (Japanese; also *hōsen*), Dharma encounter; public *dokusan*.

shūnyatā: empty infinity; infinite emptiness; the great void.

tao: (Chinese), the way or path; Dharma; prajnā; (Japanese, *dō* or *michi*).

tathatā: thusness; suchness.

teishō: (Japanese), presentation of the call; the Dharma discourse of the *rōshi*.

udumbara: a plant that blooms once every three thousand years, representing the rare appearance of the Buddha.

ukiyo: (Japanese), floating world; waves of cause and effect, birth and death; this transient life; samsāra.

zazen: (Japanese), sitting in meditation; Zen meditation.

zendō: (Japanese), meditation hall; dōjō.

Japanese Equivalents of Chinese Names

Ch'ang-sha Ching-ts'en: Chōsa Keijin
Chao-chou Ts'ung-shen: Jōshu Jūshin
Chu-chih (also Chu-ti): Gutei
Feng-hsueh Yen-chao: Fuketsu Enshō
Hang-chou T'ien-lung: Kōshū Tenryū
Hsiang-yen Chih-hsien: Kyōgen Chikan
Hsueh-tou Ch'ung-hsien: Setchō Jūken
Huang-po Hsi-yun: Ōbaku Kiun
Kao-an Ta-yu: Kōan Daigu
Kuei-shan Ling-yu: Isan Reiyū
Lin-chi I-hsuan: Rinzai Gigen
Liu T'ieh-mo: Ryū Tetsuma
Ma-tzu Tao-i: Baso Dōitsu
Nan-ch'uan P'u-yuan: Nansen Fugan
Nan-yang Hui-chung (Kuo-shih): Nan'yō Echū (Kokushi)
Nan-yueh Huai-jang: Nangaku Ejō
Pai-chang (also Po-chang) Huai-hai: Hyakujō Ekai

Ta-hui Tsung-kao: Daie Sōko
Ta-lung Chih-hung: Dairyū (*also* Dairyō) Chikō
Ta-yu: *see* Kao-an Ta-yu
T'ien-lung: *see* Hang-chou T'ien-lung
Tung-shan Liang-chieh: Tōzan Ryōkai
Tung-shan Shou-ch'u: Tōzan Shusho
Wu-men Hui-k'ai: Mumon Ekai
Yang-shan Hui-chi: Kyōzan Ejaku
Yen-t'ou Ch'uan-huo: Gantō Zenkatsu
Yun-chu Tao-ying: Ungo Dōyō
Yun-men Wen-yen: Unmon Bun'en

Notes

IN QUOTING FROM the *Wu Men Kuan* (Mumonkan; The Gateless Barrier), I have cited Kōun Yamada, "The Gateless Barrier" (tentative title), a manuscript scheduled to be published in 1979 by the Zen Center of Los Angeles, 905 South Normandie Avenue, Los Angeles, California 90006. References may also be checked by case number in Zenkei Shibayama, *Zen Comments on the Mumonkan,* New York, 1974, and in Katsuki Sekida, trans., *Two Zen Classics: Mumonkan and Hekiganroku,* New York and Tokyo, 1977.

In quoting from the *Pi Yen Lu* (Hekiganroku; The Blue Cliff Record), the *Ts'ung Jung Lu* (Shōyōroku; The Book of Equanimity), and the *Denkōroku* (Transmission of the Light), I have cited unpublished manuscripts by Kōun Yamada and Robert Aitken on file at the Maui Zendo, R. R. 1, Box 702, Haiku, Hawaii 96708. References to the *Pi Yen Lu* may be checked by case number in Thomas and J. C. Clearly, *The Blue Cliff Record,* 3 vols., Boulder and London, 1977. The *Ts'ung Jung Lu* is being translated for publication at the Zen Center of Los Angeles. Somecases cited from the *Denkōroku* are not included in the partial version found in Jiyu Kennett, *Selling Water by the River,* New York, 1972.

Introduction

1. Shaku Sōen, *Zenkai Ichiran Kōwa* (Lectures on One Wave of the Zen Sea), 2nd. ed., Tokyo, 1929.

2. R. H. Blyth, *A History of Haiku,* 2 vols., Tokyo, 1963–4, 1:110. See also Satō Madoka, *Bashō to Bukkyō* (Bashō and Buddhism), Tokyo, 1970, pp. 58–59, 193–206.

3. Yaichiro Isobe, trans., *Oku no Hosomichi, or The Poetical Journey in Old Japan, by Bashō,* Tokyo, 1933?, p. 8 fn.; notes, p. 4.

4. Donald Keene, *Landscapes and Portraits,* Tokyo and Palo Alto, 1971, pp. 123–24.

5. Makoto Ueda, *Matsuo Bashō,* New York, 1970.

6. *Ibid.,* pp. 19–35.

7. *Ibid.,* pp. 69–111.

8. See Kōun Yamada, "The Gateless Barrier," case 1, verse.

9. Taizō Ebara et al., eds., *Bashō Kōza* (Lectures on Bashō), 9 vols., Tokyo, 1943–51; also Komiya Toyotaka, *Kōhon Bashō Zenshū* (Bashō's Complete Writings: Corrected Text), 10 vols., Tokyo, 1959–69.

Chapter One

1. Kōun Yamada, "Wu Men Kuan: Case 3," *teishō* at the Maui Zendo, Haiku, Hawaii, October 28, 1971.

2. Robert Aitken, "Bashō's Haiku and Zen," M.A. dissertation, University of Hawaii, 1950, p. 89.

3. Daisetz T. Suzuki, *Sengai: The Zen Master,* Greenwich, Conn., 1971, p. 176.

4. Daisetz Teitaro Suzuki, *Essays in Zen Buddhism,* first series, London, 1949, p. 243.

5. Kōun Yamada and Robert Aitken, trans., "Shōyōroku," Maui Zendo, Haiku, Hawaii, case 67.

6. Kenneth Yasuda, *The Japanese Haiku,* Tokyo and Rutland, 1957, p. 169.

7. Yamada and Aitken, trans., "Shōyōroku," case 79. See Yamada, "The Gateless Barrier," case 46.

Chapter Two

1. Kōun Yamada, "Eihei Kōroku, fasc. 1, case 35," *teishō* at San'un Zendō, Kamakura, Japan, April 14, 1974. See *Sōtōshū Zensho* (Complete Works of the Sōtō Sect), 20 vols., Tokyo, 1930–38, 1:50. Yamada's translation.
2. Senkichiro Katsumata, gen. ed., *Kenkyusha's New Japanese-English Dictionary*, Tokyo, 1954, p. 1249.
3. R. H. Blyth, *Haiku,* 4 vols., Tokyo, 1949–52, 2:304.
4. See Suzuki, *Essays in Zen Buddhism,* first series, p. 192 ff. and pp. 363–76.
5. Related by Nakagawa Sōen Rōshi, Hara, Japan, 1951.
6. Yamada, "The Gateless Barrier," case 3.

Chapter Three

1. Blyth, *Haiku,* 3:122.
2. Donald Keene, *Landscapes and Portraits,* p. 110.
3. Nobuyuki Yuasa, *Bashō: The Narrow Road to the Deep North and Other Travel Sketches,* Baltimore, 1966, p. 95.
4. Robert Aitken, trans., "Hakuin Zenji's 'Song of Zazen'," "Daily Sutras of the Diamond Sangha" (mimeographed sutra book of the Maui and Koko An zendos), Maui Zendo, Haiku, Hawaii. Cf. Daisetz Teitaro Suzuki, *Manual of Zen Buddhism,* London, 1950, pp. 151–52.
5. *Ibid.*
6. Asataro Miyamori, *An Anthology of Haiku: Ancient and Modern,* Tokyo, 1932, p. 522 (Japanese text, my translation).
7. Shao Chang Lee, *Popular Buddhism in China,* Shanghai, 1939, p. 22 (Chinese text, my translation).
8. Miyamori, *An Anthology of Haiku,* p. 20.
9. Robert Burnett, *The Life of Paul Gauguin,* New York, 1937, p. 208 and facing illus.

Chapter Four

1. Matsuo Bashō, "Oi no Kobumi" (Records of a Travel Worn Satchel), in Ebara, *Bashō Kōza*, 8:129.

2. Yamada, "Eihei Kōroku, fasc. 1, case 35." *Sōtōshū Zensho*, 1:50.

3. See Richard B. Pilgrim, "The Religio-Aesthetic of Matsuo Bashō," *The Eastern Buddhist*, n. s., vol. 10, n. 1, May 1977, pp. 37–38.

4. Donald Keene, *Anthology of Japanese Literature*, New York, 1955, p. 370.

5. Paolo Soleri, "Relative Poverty and Frugality," *The CoEvolution Quarterly*, no. 6, 1975, p. 119.

6. Kōun Yamada and Robert Aitken, trans., "Hekiganroku," Maui Zendo, Haiku, Hawaii, case 53.

7. Yamada, "The Gateless Barrier," case 1; Philip Kapleau, *The Three Pillars of Zen*, New York and Tokyo, 1965, pp. 71–82; Zenkei Shibayama, *Zen Comments on the Mumonkan*, New York, 1974, pp. 19–31; and Durand Kiefer, "What Is Mu?" in *What Is Meditation?* ed. John White, Garden City, 1974, pp. 139–48.

Chapter Five

1. T. S. Eliot, "Preludes I," *Collected Poems 1909–1962*, New York, 1963, p. 13.

2. Dōgen Kigen, "Fukan Zazengi" (Universal Promulgation of Zazen), *Shōbōgenzō* (Treasury of the True Eye of the Dharma), trans. Kōun Yamada, "Miscellaneous Koans" (mimeographed leaflet of the Maui and Koko An zendos), Maui Zendo, Haiku, Hawaii. See Norman Waddell and Masao Abe, trans., "Fukan Zazengi," *The Eastern Buddhist*, n. s., vol. 6, no. 2, October 1973, p. 125.

3. Harold G. Henderson, *An Introduction to Haiku*, Garden City, 1958, p. 48.

4. Yamada, "The Gateless Barrier," case 16.

Chapter Six

1. Yamada and Aitken, trans., "Hekiganroku," case 1.

2. *Ibid.*, case 84.

3. Suzuki, *Manual of Zen Buddhism,* frontispiece.

4. Robert Aitken, trans., "Hannya Shingyō," "Daily Sutras of the Diamond Sangha" (Maui Zendo, Haiku, Hawaii). See Suzuki, *Manual of Zen Buddhism,* pp. 26–30.

5. Robert Aitken, trans., "Mealtime Sutras of the Diamond Sangha" (mimeographed leaflet of the Maui and Koko An zendos), Maui Zendo, Haiku, Hawaii. Cf. Jiyu Kennett, *Selling Water by the River,* New York, 1972, p. 234.

6. Aitken, "Hannya Shingyō." See Suzuki, *Manual of Zen Buddhism,* pp. 26–30.

7. Kōun Yamada, trans., personal instruction, Kamakura, San'un Zendō, June 1, 1973.

8. Suzuki, *Manual of Zen Buddhism,* p. 14.

9. Gary Snyder, *Earth House Hold,* New York, 1969, p. 10.

Chapter Seven

1. Joyce Carol Oates, "That," *The Nation,* vol. 225, no. 1, July 2, 1977, p. 23.

2. R. H. Blyth, *Zen in English Literature and Oriental Classics,* Tokyo, 1942, p. 49; *Haiku,* 3:153, *A History of Haiku,* 1:127.

3. Aitken, trans., "Mealtime Sutras of the Diamond Sangha." Cf. Kennett, *Selling Water by the River,* p. 236.

4. Yamada, "The Gateless Barrier," case 1; Kapleau, *Three Pillars,* pp. 71–82; Shibayama, *Zen Comments on the Mumonkan,* pp. 19–31; Kiefer, "What Is Mu?" in *What Is Meditation?* pp. 139–48.

5. Yamada, "The Gateless Barrier," case 18.

6. Simone Weil, *Waiting for God,* New York, 1974, pp. 107–8.

7. Blyth, *Haiku,* 3:167.

8. Sanki Ichikawa, gen. ed., *Haikai and Haiku,* Tokyo, 1958, p. 8.

9. Henderson, *An Introduction to Haiku,* p. 48.

10. Yuasa, *Bashō: The Narrow Road to the Deep North and Other Travel Sketches,* p. 46.

11. George Birbeck Hill, ed., *Boswell's Life of Johnson,* 6 vols., Oxford, 1887, 1:453.

12. W. S. Merwin, *The Miner's Pale Children,* New York, 1976, pp. 36–45.

13. Yasutani Hakuun, *Goi, Sanki, Sanjū, Jūjūkinkai Dokugo* (Soliloquy

on the Five Degrees, the Three Conversions, the Three-Fold Gathering, and the Ten Grave Precepts), Tokyo, 1962, p. 121.

Chapter Eight

1. Nobutsuna Sasaki, et al., eds., *The Manyōshū: One Thousand Poems Selected and Translated from the Japanese,* Tokyo, 1940, p. 215.

2. Miyamori, *An Anthology of Haiku,* Tokyo, 1932, p. 215.

3. Blyth, *Haiku,* 1:163.

4. Yamada and Aitken, trans., "Hekiganroku," case 6.

5. Yasutani Hakuun, *Hekiganshū Dokugo* (Soliloquy on the Blue Cliff Record), Tokyo, 1960, p. 39.

6. Paul Reps, *Zen Flesh Zen Bones,* Rutland and Tokyo, 1957, p. 82.

Chapter Nine

1. Daisetz T. Suzuki, "The Morning Glory," *The Way,* vol. 2, no. 6, p. 3, November 1950; and vol. 3, no. 1, January 1951.

2. *Ibid.*

3. *Ibid.*

4. *Ibid.,* pp. 3–4.

5. Miyamori, *An Anthology of Haiku,* p. 424.

6. Suzuki, "The Morning Glory," p. 1.

7. *Ibid.*

8. See the haiku "How Noble . . . ," p. 104; "Come," p. 142; and "Horse Chestnuts," p. 145.

9. Hatori Kōseki, *Bashō Kushū Shinkō* (New Studies in the Poetical Works of Bashō), 2 vols., Tokyo, 1932, 2:704.

10. Yamada and Aitken, trans., "Hekiganroku," case 82.

Chapter Ten

1. Sanki Ichikawa, gen. ed., *Haikai and Haiku,* p. 11.

2. Ueda, *Matsuo Bashō,* p. 61.

3. Miyamori, *An Anthology of Haiku,* p. 211.

4. Ueda, *Matsuo Bashō,* p. 115 ff.

5. Yamada and Aitken, trans., "Hekiganroku," case 51.

6. Yasutani Hakuun, *Mumonkan Dokugo* (Soliloquy on the Gateless Barrier), Tokyo, 1956, p. 7.

7. Daisetz Teitaro Suzuki, *Essays in Zen Buddhism*, second series, London, 1950, p. 248.

8. Yamada and Aitken, "Hekiganroku," case 26.

9. Yasutani Hakuun, *Hekiganshū Dokugo*, p. 152.

10. See Yamada and Aitken, trans., "Hekiganroku," case 57.

11. "Shobogenzo Genjo Koan: An Analytic Study," Zen Center, San Francisco, n.d., Japanese text and literal translation, p. 8.

Chapter Eleven

1. Yamada, "The Gateless Barrier," case 35, verse.

2. See Chapter 12, p. 94.

3. Isshū Miura and Ruth Fuller Sasaki, *Zen Dust*, New York, 1966, p. 181. See Chapter 26.

4. Blyth, *Haiku*, 4:xi.

5. Suzuki, *Essays in Zen Buddhism*, first series, p. 333 fn.

6. Norman Waddell and Masao Abe, "Genjō Kōan," *The Eastern Buddhist*, n.s., vol. 5, no. 2, October, 1972, p. 130.

7. Sōen Nakagawa, "Dedication," "Daily Sutras of the Diamond Sangha."

Chapter Twelve

1. Kakuzo Okakura, *The Book of Tea*, Tokyo, 1939, pp. 24, 51.

2. Daisetz T. Suzuki, *Zen and Japanese Culture*, New York, 1959, p. 280.

3. Shin'ichi Hisamatsu, *Zen and the Fine Arts*, trans. Gishin Tokiwa, Tokyo and Palo Alto, 1971, pp. 25–27.

4. R. H. Blyth, "Buddhism and Haiku," *Monumenta Nipponica*, vol. 7, no. 1/2, 1951, p. 213.

5. Weil, *Waiting for God*, p. 115.

6. Yamada and Aitken, trans., "Hekiganroku," case 24.

Chapter Thirteen

1. This information and the haiku itself may be fiction. Some scholars believe that Bashō constructed *The Narrow Road Within* as a series of linked essays based on conventions of renku, which required at least one reference, however distant, to sexual love. It is thought that perhaps Bashō was more faithful here to literary form than to the facts. Ueda, *Matsuo Bashō*, pp. 138–44.
2. Keene, *Anthology of Japanese Literature*, pp. 372–73.
3. Miyamori, *An Anthology of Haiku*, pp. 148–49.
4. Ueda, *Matsuo Bashō*, pp. 57–58.
5. Yamada, ''The Gateless Barrier,'' case 26.
6. Matt. 7:1.

Chapter Fourteen

1. Nakagawa, ''Dedication.''
2. Chung-yuan Chang, *Original Teachings of Ch'an Buddhism*, New York, 1969, p. 46.
3. Kōun Yamada, ''The Stature of Yasutani Hakuun Rōshi,'' Kōun Yamada and Robert Aitken, trans., *The Eastern Buddhist*, n. s., vol. 7, no. 2, October 1974, pp. 114–15.
4. Blyth, *Haiku*, 1:205.

Chapter Fifteen

1. Yamada and Aitken, trans., ''Hekiganroku,'' case 11.
2. *Ibid.*, case 69.
3. Kōun Yamada, ''The Gateless Barrier,'' case 15.
4. Edited from Suzuki, *Essays in Zen Buddhism*, first ser., p. 221, fn.
5. Yamada and Aitken, trans., ''Hekiganroku,'' case 36.

Chapter Sixteen

1. Blyth, Haiku, 4:262.
2. R. H. Blyth, *Senryu: Japanese Satirical Verses*, Tokyo, 1949, p. 76.

3. Eidō Shimano and Robert Aitken, trans., "Shōdōka" (Song of Realization), "Daily Sutras of the Diamond Sangha" (mimeographed leaflet of the Maui and Koko An zendos), Maui Zendo, Haiku, Hawaii. See Nyogen Senzaki, *Buddhism and Zen,* New York, 1953, p. 65.

4. See Suzuki, *Essays in Zen Buddhism,* second series, pp. 47–48.

5. Yamada and Aitken, trans., "Shōyōroku," case 54.

Chapter Seventeen

1. Blyth, *Haiku,* 4:316.

2. Suzuki, *Essays in Zen Buddhism,* second series, facing p. 81.

3. Kōun Yamada and Robert Aitken, trans., "Denkōroku," Maui Zendo, Haiku, Hawaii, case 6, verse.

4. Yanagida Seizan, gen. ed. *Teihon Rinzai Zenji Goroku* (Sayings of Zen Master Lin-chi, Authenticated Text), Tokyo, 1971, pp. 62–63, 126. See Ruth Fuller Sasaki, *The Recorded Sayings of Ch'an Master Lin-chi Hui-chao of Chen Prefecture,* Kyoto, 1975, p. 54.

5. See Yamada and Aitken, trans., "Denkōroku," case 51. Cf. Chapter 10, note 11.

6. Shibayama, *Zen Comments on the Mumonkan,* p. 332.

7. Yaichiro Isobe, trans., *Musings of a Chinese Vegetarian,* Tokyo, 1925, p. 64.

Chapter Eighteen

1. Blyth, *Haiku,* 1:378.

2. Burton Watson, *The Complete Works of Chuang Tzu,* New York, 1968, p. 49.

3. *Ibid.,* p. 43.

4. *Ibid.*

5. Yoel Hoffman, *The Sound of One Hand,* New York, 1975.

6. Watson, *Chuang Tzu,* pp. 47–48.

7. *Ibid.,* p. 48.

8. Yamada, "The Gateless Barrier," case 10, verse.

9. *Ibid.,* case 25.

10. Cited by Kōun Yamada, personal instruction San'un Zendō, Kamakura, Japan, April 20, 1974.

11. Lee, *Popular Buddhism in China,* p. 22.

Chapter Nineteen

1. Edited from Yamada, "The Gateless Barrier," case 24.

2. *Ibid.,* case 22, verse.

3. James Norman Hall, "December in the Tropics," *The Atlantic Monthly,* vol. 157, no. 4, April 1936, p. 500.

4. Robert Louis Stevenson, "To S. R. Crockett," *Poems and Ballads,* New York, 1907, p. 272.

Chapter Twenty

1. Blyth, *Haiku,* 4:91.

2. Sōen Nakagawa, inscription on a tray, author's collection.

3. Katō Shishū (pseud.), ed., *Haijin Buson Zenden* (Complete Heritage of the Haiku Poet Buson), Tokyo, 1937, p. 398. See Blyth, *Haiku,* 3:251.

4. Robert S. De Ropp, *The Master Game,* New York, 1968.

5. Yamada and Aitken, trans., "Hekiganroku," case 84.

6. Suzuki, *Manual of Zen Buddhism,* frontispiece.

7. Blyth, *Haiku,* 3:280.

8. Yamada and Aitken, trans., "Hekiganroku," case 18.

Chapter Twenty-one

1. Blyth, *A History of Haiku,* 1:128.

2. Miyamori, *An Anthology of Haiku,* p. 117.

3. Daisetz Teitaro Suzuki, "Human Values in Zen," *The Essentials of Zen,* ed. Bernard Phillips, London, 1963, p. 42.

4. Nyoten Jimbo, *Mumonkan Kōwa* (Lectures on the Gateless Barrier), Tokyo, 1946, p. 42.

5. Yamada, "The Gateless Barrier," case 21.

6. Robert Louis Stevenson, *Fables,* New York, 1896, p. 74.

Chapter Twenty-two

1. Ebara, *Bashō Kōza*, 2:223.
2. Fumiko Fujikawa, "The Influence of Tu Fu on Bashō," *Monumenta Nipponica*, vol. 20, no. 3/4, 1965, pp. 380–81.
3. *Ibid.*
4. *Ibid.*, p. 381.
5. Yamada and Aitken, trans., "Hekiganroku," case 40.
6. Fujikawa, "The Influence of Tu Fu on Bashō," p. 382.

Chapter Twenty-three

1. Yuasa, *Bashō: The Narrow Road to the Deep North and Other Travel Sketches*, p. 83.
2. Miyamori, *An Anthology of Haiku*, p. 111.
3. Nhat Hanh, *The Miracle of Being Awake*, Nyack, N. Y., 1975, pp. 9–10.
4. *Ibid.*, p. 6.
5. Suzuki, *Essays in Zen Buddhism*, first series, pp. 236–37.
6. Yamada and Aitken, trans., "Shōyōroku," case 77.

Chapter Twenty-four

1. Toshijiro Hirayama, "Seasonal Rituals Connected with Rice Culture," *Studies in Japanese Folklore*, ed. Richard M. Dorson, Bloomington, Ind., 1963, pp. 67–68.
2. Yamada and Aitken, trans., "Hekiganroku," case 18.

Chapter Twenty-five

1. James H. Murray, et al., eds., *A New English Dictionary on Historical Principles*, 10 vols., Oxford and New York, 1888–1928, 1:988.
2. Kōun Yamada, trans., personal instruction, Koko An Zendo, Honolulu, February 22, 1972.
3. Yamada, "The Gateless Barrier," case 2.
4. Kōun Yamada, personal instruction, Maui Zendo, Haiku, Hawaii, November 1, 1971.

Chapter Twenty-six

1. Cited by Ebara, *Bashō Kōza,* 3:161–62.

2. *Ibid.*

3. *Ibid.*

4. *Ibid.*

5. Yasutani Hakuun, personal instruction, Maui Zendo, Haiku, Hawaii, October 15, 1969.

6. Walt Whitman, "Song of Myself," *Leaves of Grass,* New York, 1958, p. 74.

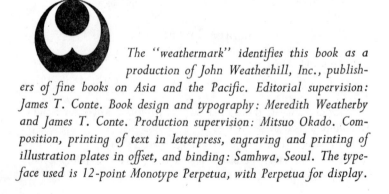

The "weathermark" identifies this book as a production of John Weatherhill, Inc., publishers of fine books on Asia and the Pacific. Editorial supervision: James T. Conte. Book design and typography: Meredith Weatherby and James T. Conte. Production supervision: Mitsuo Okado. Composition, printing of text in letterpress, engraving and printing of illustration plates in offset, and binding: Samhwa, Seoul. The typeface used is 12-point Monotype Perpetua, with Perpetua for display.